THE WORLD
OF THE VOICE-OVER

This book is dedicated to Sylvia for her unrelenting help
over the past thirty years.

The World
of the Voice-Over

*Writing, adapting and translating scripts; training the
voice; building a studio*

by

Daniel Pageon

Actors World
Production Ltd

British Library Cataloguing in Publication Data
A catalogue record for this book is available from the British Library.

ISBN 978-0-9554487-0-6

Typeset by Amolibros, Milverton, Somerset
This book production has been managed by Amolibros
Printed and bound by T J International Ltd, Padstow, Cornwall, UK

CONTENTS

ACKNOWLEDGMENTS

I would like to thank the Institute of Translation and Interpreting, and the Chartered Institute of Linguists for giving me the opportunity to lecture on this subject. I also would like to thank Sylvia who encouraged me to put pen to paper and then supported me all the way through. Many colleagues, translators and "voices" gave me material for this work, including Tom Wesel who sent me "Why I write" by George Orwell, Young Lee and Hiroko Iida who gave me the Korean and Japanese examples, Ewa Piotrowska and Deborah Chan for the tongue-twisters in Polish and in Chinese. I would also like to thank Lara Parmiani, who is an actress as well as a voice coach, for her input. Thanks to PK Studios for letting me take pictures of their Atari and to Charlie Dodd for helping on technical terminology; and to Rowan Laxton of Alchemy who assisted me in the first stages of building the studio; and Joel Schrire who combined his knowledge of IT with his skills as a sound engineer to make the studio work smoothly. I would also like to thank Joanna Clarkson with whom I worked on subtitles for over fifteen years and who helped me with that chapter. I would also like to thank Absolut Vodka, Krohne, Televisionary and SKF, the clients who let me use extracts from their scripts to illustrate specific issues we encounter in translating. Special thanks to Moira Babary for her insight into The Alexander Technique, which she has been teaching for many years, and to Katherine Begley, Sophie Pageon and Christopher Kent for revising my draft.

PICTURE CREDITS

FOREWORD

If you intend to try the world of voice-over, then this book is a must.

Of course it is not the first, or the only volume that has been written about this arcane, challenging, sometimes frustrating, potentially rewarding, and wonderful activity. Indeed, doing voice-overs is one of the most coveted of jobs. Many people are seduced by its (apparent) glamour; some imagine it is easy, others dream of the wealth it will undoubtedly bring them. When a "hopeful" approaches me for tips or guidance, I always ask why they think they will make a good voice-over. Frequently the answer is "so-and-so says I have a good voice."

Sorry, that is not enough. I am telling you, and so will Daniel tell you in this book.

But do not be alarmed, dismayed or put off. If someone recognises that you have a specific ability or talent, it's only natural to want to use it, share it, develop it, and maybe (with a lot of luck, a considerable amount of ability, and a load of hard work) even make a career out of it.

Which brings us to this splendid volume.

Daniel Pageon has much more than "a considerable amount of ability", and has made language and voice-over a large part of his life.

The first part of the book covers the specific requirements of a translator – and some of the pitfalls awaiting him or her. Do not be put off by this, if you are just expecting hints about being a voice-over in your own language. (I was going to say "in English", but knowing Daniel as I do, he'll probably translate this whole book into German, French, Italian and several other tongues!)

The book does not get bogged down with enormous or unnecessary detail at any stage, but addresses the areas you will want, and need, to know if you are serious about the world of the voice-over.

It has been written by a vastly experienced, knowledgeable and delightful man, who specialises in communication. As he says, he started writing it as "a talk", and therefore you will not be surprised to find it easy to read.

Enjoy this book, and I wish you success with the luck, ability and hard work that may lie ahead of you!

Patrick Lunt
December 2006

INTRODUCTION

My aim in this "talk" is to try to help "traditional" translators become translators of the **spoken** word as a first stage and then ultimately become "voice-overs" themselves. I will even talk them through building their home recording studio. The spoken word covers a number of production types. The most common one is the "voice-over", and as our society evolves from a system of communication on paper to one based on oral communication there are more and more opportunities for translators to work on this type of translation. For example, all sorts of surveys that used to require the ticking of boxes on paper questionnaires are now conducted over the phone, with a computer at the other end recording the answers. There is also an enormous amount of material produced on CD, CD-ROM or DVD to train people. In many cases they are multilingual productions and therefore require the work of translators at one stage or another. I cover even more specialised translations as well, for example when actors appearing on the screen need to be synched.

Another area of interest is the subtitling of films. Subtitling is more common in certain languages than others. This is a type of translation that is **written**, but it is also subject to length constraints which are not too dissimilar to those imposed when translating "voice-overs".

I also describe what "voice-overs" do and how translators can become voice artists as well. I will try to suggest criteria by which translators and actors can assess their potential and then describe the training that they will need to go through to be able to read professionally.

I examine what IT can do to help us in our daily work as

translators and "voices". There is a chapter on marketing our services, including making a demo and the all-important subject of fees. I also touch on teambuilding, which might surprise some freelance people, such as translators, used to working on their own.

I end with a chapter on the work of Frederick Matthias Alexander, the Australian actor who lost his voice and created a technique widely used today to help not only performers, but the public at large to lead a better life through respect for their bodies.

BIOGRAPHY

Daniel Pageon was brought up in the French Air Force, which his father joined when Daniel was only nine months old. The first postings were in Provence, Nîmes and Aix-en-Provence. A long journey through different countries ensued. Morocco, Mali, Senegal and Morocco again before quite a few postings in France: Marseilles, Bordeaux, Bourges and then back to Provence. That also meant a spell in seventeen different schools and Daniel occasionally totted up three schools in a single school year, including one in a tiny village near Lyon. His best subject at school was *récitation*. He loved, not so much the learning of the poems, as their presentation in

front of a captive audience. To spur him on in his early days he even got a standing ovation from teenagers for reciting a poem in prose by one of the *poètes maudits* Tristan Corbière about Brittany, when he was but a teenager himself! His great skill at recitation was not quite enough to pass the *Baccalauréat* but luck was on his side as he took the dreaded *Bac* after the May 1968 revolution. That year almost nobody failed!

However, Daniel didn't entirely waste his time at school. He did well in the subjects he liked: French literature and history. To complement this formal way of learning things he also spent a lot of time at the local MJC (*Maison des Jeunes et de la Culture*) where, under the direction of Philippe Trouvé,[1] he studied drama very seriously over a period of two years.

As for many other young people across Europe, 1968 was a pivotal year in his life. The French university Daniel hoped to attend did not open in October of that year, but he had a Plan B. Daniel put on his rucksack and hitchhiked to London to taste the Swinging Sixties and get to grips with the language of Shakespeare. Of course, like all students of English of that generation he was more familiar with Hamlet's speech than he was with ordering a coffee or asking for the price of a room in a bed and breakfast. Daniel, however, found he had a gift for languages; he had done reasonably well at Arabic at primary school in Morocco but was not so successful back in France where English was taught in a way which as the French say was not *sa tasse de thé* (his cup of tea)!

Once in London he worked hard on improving his English. He started to study the language "on location", as an actor would say, and then thought he should also improve his Italian; after all, his mother was born in Italy. As a consequence of this decision Daniel spent time between London and Rome over a period of four years. By 1971 he had managed to secure his first broadcasting job at the BBC, but there was still the hurdle of National Service to negotiate. Daniel decided he was not going to waste his time in the Army like so many other youngsters, and volunteered to go to Germany as that would be a splendid opportunity to learn the language. Little did he know! German is pretty difficult and time-consuming, but Daniel found an unexpected solution to this problem. He met Sylvia in Berlin and married her and has been practising his German ever since! They have three children who are trilingual.

After his duty for "King and Country", or rather for the "République", he was offered a contract by the BBC World Service, where he learnt to become a translator and broadcaster, practising every day for five years. His translation work was supervised by

Cyril Alexander,[2] an astonishing linguist who could have taught French to the French and English to the English and was so devoted to his job that he made working in the newsroom a pleasure. After that, Daniel was ready to fly solo, making a living in the world of the spoken word.

He has recorded thousands of hours of narration for documentaries, corporate videos, training material and language courses, mainly in French but also sometimes in English, Italian, German and even Spanish, which he started to learn at evening classes. Having been asked a few times to talk about the specificity of translating for the "voice-over", he was prompted by his wife to write an essay on the subject. And, not being one to delay matters for long, he sat down in front of his computer and started typing away...

---

1   Philippe Trouvé was director of the MJC in Salon-de-Provence in the mid-sixties. A humanist versed in diverse artistic activities, he directed plays, he writes poetry and paints. One of his paintings can be seen on the Internet.

2   Cyril Alexander: 1919 – 2004. "Alex" was British but brought up in France. He worked for British Intelligence during the Second World War and for the BBC to a ripe old age, training generations of aspiring bilingual journalists.

THE WORK OF
THE TRANSLATOR

Definitions

There are a number of basic terms that need to be explained before getting into the nitty-gritty of translating the spoken word. Four words are sometimes misunderstood by outsiders, in other words mainly by clients. They are *translation, transcription, interpreting, transliteration* and their derivatives.

Translations are written, whether they are going to be read with the eyes only or spoken aloud. You find them in books, in manuals, in brochures, leaflets and on labels. If you look at labels on tins or boxes, most of you will have had a laugh at one stage or another at what you have read. That is because these short sentences have not been translated by professional translators, or if they have, the translator has been asked to do it in half a dozen languages, and of course he or she is only a native speaker of one of them. That should be enough to show people that translating is not as easy as replacing words from one language with words from another.

Interpreting is the act of translating verbally, and mostly live, a speech as it is spoken. There are three main categories:

The first one is simultaneous interpretation, such as those carried out at international conferences at the United Nations or in Brussels, for example. These require highly trained individuals who are able to listen to one language and speak in another, not more than a few seconds behind the original speaker. These interpreters normally work in pairs and use a booth which is equipped to let them hear the original speech through headphones and a microphone into which they speak the foreign language. They work in pairs because they cannot last for much more than about twenty minutes without taking a break, and even during the break they might be required to help their colleague. Sometimes an interpreter might get stuck on a word and require his or her colleague's help. Of course, speakers who are used to speaking at international conferences try not to speak too fast unless, that is, they have an ulterior motive or they aren't aware of exactly what is going on in the little cubicles at the end of the room.

The second category is consecutive interpreting. This is when the speaker speaks one sentence or two and the interpreter repeats the same sentence in the foreign language. Some speakers will make the work of the interpreter a bit easier by using short sentences and stopping to give time for the message to be relayed in the foreign tongue, but they don't all do it that way!

The third is the whispering technique. You might have seen this happening when, for example, heads of state meet and they have someone in between them who whispers in their ear. Usually, important dignitaries have their own interpreters and since they know each other well, the interpreting job is a little bit easier.

Interpreters, as I said earlier, are highly trained; they very often have to work in two directions. In the old days, budding interpreters had to speak four languages fluently before they could even start training to become interpreters. Nowadays, because the demand has increased so much in international institutions, that number of languages has been reduced, but they must still be outstanding linguists to do this very demanding job.

The two techniques, *translating* and *interpreting*, try to achieve the same aim of making sure a non-speaker of a language can understand what the other person is saying. They make communication possible between people who would otherwise not be able to understand each other. The techniques, as I have tried to explain briefly, are very different and require different skills.

Transcribing is a job best done by an audio typist. This will be explained in detail later on. Transcribing is the act of putting on paper what someone is saying. In our field it mainly happens with interviews. The translation is then done after the speech has been transcribed.

As for *transliteration*, this is what is done when foreign words using a different alphabet or pictograms are written using the Roman alphabet. It is a sort of phonetic writing. This can cause some problems to translators as well. The transliteration of some names will not be spelt the same in English and in French or Spanish. Just a couple of examples: in Spanish the word football is used but written "fútbol". This is the transliteration of the word. Sometimes a name like the name of the Russian composer will be spelt Glazunov in English and Glazounov in French, simply because the sound "u" in English is represented in French by the letters "ou". It happens of course all the time between languages that do not use the same alphabet. However, there is a worrying trend in France, through pure laziness on the part of the journalist, not to say lack of knowledge, to use the English spelling for transliteration, which of course does not really make any sense at all!

The technical parameters

There are a number of technical parameters that have to be taken into consideration when translating for a "voice-over". (The "**voice-over**" is the action of voicing over the picture; it is also the result of that action. It is a narration and the **narrator** is also known as a "**voice-over**" or even a "**voice**" for short. In the business there are other words describing this profession like "**voice actor**"; we also refer to them simply as "**artists**". The Americans talk about a "**talent**" when they want to book one of my "voices" for example.) The technical parameters are the differences that need to be considered between translating for a book, a magazine or a manual and translating a script that will be "mouthed" by an artist. The first difference arises from the constraints dictated by length.

Spoken versus written

People who are not translators very often do not quite understand what translating entails. Some clients think it is just a question of replacing words from one language with words from another language. Well, translators know that this is not the case. There are many types of translation, but to achieve a good translation you need to understand all the subtleties of the source language as well as the target language. Not only do you need to have a thorough knowledge of what I would call the technicalities of the language, the vocabulary and syntax, but also of the cultures of the two languages. You need to add to that the understanding of the subject matter. If translating were only a question of replacing words from one language with another, computers could do it quite efficiently, and we would all be out of work – but they cannot (yet). Human input is still extremely important when doing most, if not all, translations. There are tools on the market, some accessible through the Internet, that claim to be able to translate, but the results tend to be so poor that very often the resulting translation is not understandable. There are many types of translations. One cannot compare the work of a translator of poetry to a translator of technical manuals! And then there is also the difference between what is required to translate for the **written** word and the **spoken** word.

For the **spoken** word I must emphasize that you must **not** write as if your work was going to be printed in a manual or a magazine. I do insist on that: it seems to be quite obvious to me, but I have been confronted so often with translations which have been written to be read and not spoken, that I need to turn the spotlight on this one aspect of these types of translations. You will probably already have noticed that the way I **write** here is not the way **you** would write; it is on paper, but really I am **speaking** to you. It is indeed what you will have to try to achieve in your own language; you will need to become conscious of the difference between the **written** and the **spoken** word. To do that, the best way is to speak your translation aloud; it is easier of course if you work on your own! And do not read it *"dans votre barbe"* as we say in French, in other words do not mumble the words; you need to articulate them well. You might find out later on that this added work might become quite beneficial to your future as a voice-over yourself. Another big plus of speaking the words aloud is that you will realise that some words "sound" better than others. A word might technically be right, but it might not sound very good, for all sorts of reasons; it could be the sound itself, and that of course could be subjective. It is not unlike translating, or writing poetry or work of a literary nature. The look of words on paper is important, but their sound when spoken is also important and must be taken into consideration. A word could bring associations that would not be suitable or might be distracting and of course it could sound like another word (a homonym) and be misleading. In writing there might not be any confusion in the reader's mind in such a case, but when spoken all sorts of things could happen. Some simple words could bring to the listener's mind a picture totally irrelevant to the subject matter.

When that sort of thing happens while reading an article, it isn't a problem as you can pause, think about it, have a good laugh, and restart at the beginning of the sentence. However, with the spoken word, the result would be that the listener could be distracted and therefore part of the message would be lost, so be careful here as well. In most cases the listener will not rewind to listen to the bits he didn't in fact hear. It is a bit like when you read a book at night in bed, it is very late, your eyes are going through the motions and you suddenly realise that you have "seen" three pages, but that you haven't got a clue what they were all about. Well, you put the book down and you can restart the next day. The same sort of thing happens when you are distracted while listening to a voice, but the difference is you can't go back. You wouldn't stand up in a room of a hundred people and ask for the tape to be played back — well, unless it was so bad that everybody agreed with you, a very unlikely situation you must admit. People are either too polite or think it is only themselves who did not get it!

Now, another factor to take into consideration is the audience you are addressing. That is probably the same as with a written translation, but it is still worth remembering that you are not likely to address, say, an assembly of doctors on the advantages of using a new drug in quite the same way as you would, for example, a group of mechanics who need to learn how to change a part in an engine. The most important thing is not to sound condescending to your audience. I am using the example of mechanics because cars are becoming so sophisticated nowadays that they require a lot of knowledge on the part of the mechanics who therefore need to be trained thoroughly to ensure our cars behave like clockwork. I must say that to find the right level at which to 'talk' is probably the most difficult aspect of our work. The choice of words is very important. I remember using a word once in French which I thought was totally right, it was the word *péripatétitienne* which comes from the Greek and means to walk about. The Greek philosopher Aristotle used to teach while walking and that word became part of the French language. However, when I used it I had lost sight of the audience I was addressing; they were not people who knew anything about philosophy. They knew the word, oh yes! But only its popular meaning, i.e. someone walking the street, a prostitute! You will therefore need to ask your client who the target audience is and remember it while writing.

You will also need to ask if the narration is going to be read by a man or a woman. These factors have more importance in some languages than in others: they are certainly very important in Japanese, but will also make a difference in French.

Take this example:

English male or female reader	French male	French female
I have been chosen for this presentation because I am the most intelligent and most beautiful…	J'ai été choisi pour cette présentation parce que je suis le plus intelligent et le plus beau…	J'ai été choisi**e** pour cette présentation parce que je suis **la** plus intelligent**e** et **la** plus be**lle**…

Table 1

One cannot "hear" the first change « choisi**e** » but the other four are audible and therefore very important.

Even if you don't understand French you can see that they are very small changes. However, these "small" changes would make it laughable if a man was to read the female column or a woman the male column. Of course the implications and the changes in the script could be far greater and far more complex if they were cultural changes rather than mere grammatical changes, as in the case above.

In Japanese, the way you address people depends very much on the relative status of the people addressing each other. Hiroko Iida was kind enough to provide the example below:

English (Student to Teacher or Teacher to Student)	Student to Teacher	Teacher to Student
Good morning, Takeshi!	たけし先生、おはようございます。	たけし君、おはよう。

Table 2

In this very simple example above (in speaking I could not use the word "above" – I would have to say something like: "As I told you earlier", or point at a slide if it was a live presentation, or say: "as you can see on the screen", something along these lines.) So, in this example you can see the differences in dark grey and pale grey. The middle column looks longer, this is because a student would use honorific language to show his respect to the teacher, which is shown in pale grey. Speaking of respect, Japanese people put a suffix at the end of the name when they address someone unless they are on very close terms, and the suffix can be different depending on whom you're talking to – whether it's a man or a woman or if it's your teacher or sometimes it even depends on the situation. In the above example, the dark grey one shows the difference between what the student could say and what the teacher could say.

The length

Another aspect of your translation that will be problematic is the length of the sentences. Most languages, if not all, are longer than English; you will therefore need to translate the **idea** behind the sentence or the paragraph. You will very rarely have the possibility of translating all the words, as this would then take too long to read. In order to do that, I would recommend that you inform your client that you are going to be working on the script as an **editor** as much as a **translator**. It is a necessary step if you do not want to have the hassle of explaining why you have not translated every single word. This is something that tends to occur when the client has an O or A level in French, Spanish, Italian or German and gets lost in your translation because it is too good. As you have not translated word for word it becomes too difficult for the client to understand. Another suggestion is to tell your client that you would really like someone in the company or one of the distributors in the territory concerned to read the script and approve it (a native of the language you are working into is highly recommended).

When you "take liberties" with the client's script you might very well say something that is not quite right, or you might use a word or piece of jargon that happens to be used by their competitors. Now, this is additional work for your client, so you need to present it in a way that shows them it is to their advantage to go down that route. You can do that by explaining that the cost of revising the translation and reworking it is relatively small compared to having to redo part or all of the narration. That could cost hundreds of pounds if you need to call back the artist and book another hour in the studio. You could also point out that, when the original script was written, there was a "shuttle" going on between the creative director, the writer and maybe the managing director of the company and that in fact the script you are working on is version 17, so two or three versions of the translation should be considered as quite reasonable. After all, you want to help your clients present their company or message in the best possible way.

All these points need to be clarified with the client, and of course that only needs to be done the first time you work with this specific client; once they know that the process works well and to the benefit of the company, they will hopefully stick to it, says he!!!

Once you have obtained the freedom to do the translation, you need to fit it to the time codes you will have been given. But will you have been given these time codes? The best possible scenario is to have received a VHS or a DVD of the film you are translating from your client, together with an English transcript of the recorded text. The text should have the time codes in one column, so it is easy to work out how long each paragraph should be.

Narrator	Duration in seconds
In the Middle East archaeologists have found traces from distillation devices, made of terracotta, dating as far back as 3500 BC. But they weren't necessarily used to refine alcohol though. Instead they often refined essential oils and rose water. Trying to bring out the purest and most refined ingredients. Al Kuhl. Later to be known as alcohol in Europe.	00:03:51:00 – 00:04:21:00
One of the first experiments with distillation in Europe is thought to have taken place at the Salerno School in Italy in the twelfth century. Most of them behind closed doors.	00:04:26:00 – 00:04:38:00
Distillation was since long associated with alchemy and black magic. Some people even regarded the effects of the potion as supernatural.	00:04:45:00 – 00:04:58:00
A French Alchemist, Arnaud de Villeneuve, described it as "eau-de-vie – the elixir of eternal life".	00:05:03:00 – 00:05:14:00

Table 3

In this example, the script was translated into a dozen languages, including Japanese and Korean. They all had to fit the time codes as shown in the right hand column. If you look carefully, and read the script aloud yourself with your stopwatch, you will notice that this film director had enough experience of foreign language productions to give plenty of time for the translation, but that is not always the case. In this instance the translators did not see the film before doing the translation. The linguistic advisor on the project inserted the little note about the Salerno School, as for some translators far away from Europe Salerno might have been quite an obscure reference.

The length of the paragraph, however, is only one parameter in this equation. There is another issue facing the translators even when the time codes are provided: the grammatical difference between the original language and the target language. Many will know that in German the verbs are put at the end of the sentence. But I would like to take an example from the Korean where the word order is quite different. Sometimes the translator will have to change the structure of the sentence so that the words come in the right place.

As it happens, in this case the translator, Young Lee, was also the voice-over artist and had many years' experience in this field. She was quite familiar with the script and was able to make the changes in a matter of seconds in the studio. The script fitted very well as a whole because she had worked with the time codes. However, she had not seen the film and did not know that the names of the famous people mentioned had to be in a specific place in the script, as film scenes with them appeared on the screen. So the following sentence:

"The long winters have shaped generations of filmmakers and actors… **Ingmar Bergman, Max von Sydow, Greta Garbo, Anita Ekberg, Ingrid Bergman**…"

was translated in normal/traditional Korean as:

"겨울이 길다 보니 **잉마 버그만, 막스 폰 시도우, 그레타 가보, 아니타 에크버그, 잉그리드 버그만** 같은 영화제작자와 배우들을 배출하게 된 거죠."

The "back translation" gives:

"The long winters – **Ingmar Bergman, Max von Sydow, Greta Garbo, Anita Ekberg, Ingrid Bergman** – filmmakers and actors – generations – have shaped.'

As you can see the names in bold and underlined appear far too early in the sentence, and did not fit with the pictures, so the translator had to rewrite the sentence so that the names appeared towards the end of the sentence:

"겨울이 길다 보니 많은 영화제작자와 배우들을 배출하게 되었는데... **잉마 버그만, 막스 폰 시도우, 그레타 가보, 아니타 에크버그, 잉그리드 버그만** 등 입니다."

The "back translation" now looks like this:

"The long winters – numerous filmmakers and actors – generations – have shaped... – **Ingmar Bergman, Max von Sydow, Greta Garbo, Anita Ekberg, Ingrid Bergman** – such as."

Now the names are coming much closer to the original English positioning and they will appear in the right place and at the right time on the sound track. So writers must be prepared to juggle with their own language to fit the picture. This needs to be done to fit the picture, but of course the sentence must also make sense and be understandable. Once more, you realise that it is quite essential to watch the film when making the translation. In practice it does not depend on us and very often the client does not send us the film and does not even send us the time codes. So you need to use a number of tricks when you are confronted with a translation with no time codes.

If you don't have the time codes, the script you receive may look something like this:

VOICE-OVER SCRIPT
V2.0 – 10/09/01 – XY

Krohne – a symbol for quality and technical excellence in the competitive field of flow measurement.

(pause 7 seconds)

Krohne manufacture flow meters for most applications. They measure anything from oils, water, and most other liquids, through to gaseous products.

(pause)

In today's rapidly moving world, it is vital to keep *your* product and profits moving…

To keep *you* ahead, Krohne's research and development laboratories have been searching for new ways to break the barriers by the use of <u>ultrasonics</u>.

(pause)

Traditional, <u>mechanical</u>, flow meters – although popular – have several disadvantages…

By restricting the flow, they *'pressure loss'*…the moving parts are subject to wear…so the meters need to be regularly serviced and re-calibrated to maintain accuracy.

But now, these disadvantages are about to become a thing of the past!

Table 4

So here you do not have a clue as to how long you have to write each sentence. There is the mention of a seven-second pause at the beginning, but then no more reference to length and even that is not useful. You don't know if you can use this time in your translation as something very loud could be happening at this juncture on the sound track. What do you do? (The following scenario is not based on our relationship with Krohne, which has always been good.) Well, you can ask the client and you might be lucky – he will send you a time-coded script. Okay, but the secretary has gone and he cannot do it himself, you see it is five or six p.m., she has gone home and he is "all aloney on his owny"[1]. So then you tell him maybe he could send you a VHS or a DVD in the post, but of course the translation is for the following morning and there are a thousand words to translate. So being a helpful type of guy or girl, you suggest something else. Well, after all we are now in the twenty-first century. I know, I started life in the previous millennium, but I like to use the Internet and all the modern technology! So I might even ask him to send me the film through Cyberspace. It is not that difficult, he only needs to save it as an MPEG Video file and upload it to my FTP[2] site. I can open an account for him within five minutes and send him a link to do it while he makes his copy. You would be surprised, but he is very unlikely to be able to do that. "Come on, you have the script, just translate it!" He might not put it quite in these words if he is a decent chap, but he probably thinks them. So, confronted with this type of situation, you need to find a way. And the way that works pretty well for me is to create two columns:

English original	Translation
"VOICE OVER SCRIPT	"VOICE OVER SCRIPT
V2.0 – 10/09/01 – XY	V2.0 – 10/09/01 – XY
Krohne – a symbol for quality and technical excellence in the competitive field of flow measurement.	Krohne – est synonyme de qualité et d'excellence technique dans le domaine de la mesure de débit…
(pause 7 seconds)	(pause 7 seconds)
Krohne manufacture flow meters for most applications. They measure anything from oils, water, and most other liquids, through to gaseous products.	Krohne fabrica equipos de medida de caudal para la mayoría de las aplicaciones. Estos miden todo tipo de aceites, agua, y la mayor parte de otros líquidos, además de productos gaseosos.
(pause)	(pause)

Table 5

As you can see, the French is on three lines and the word "competitive" has been omitted. This is the sort of freedom you must talk about with the client. If you need to get rid of a word (if there is no space to put it in or if the narrator has to read so fast that it becomes ridiculous), then cut it, make it sound good in the translated language. Remind your client that the viewer is not going to compare what he watches with the original version. If the translation is too long, read too fast for the sake of a few words, it is not worth it. The message will be lost, the impact will be eroded and the entire purpose of the exercise will have been lost. If the translation into French had occupied five or six lines you would have known straight away that you were going to have a problem. And please don't try to be clever the way one guy did once. He just reduced the point size in the translated column!!! Don't even think about it! Don't make the translation column wider either!

I have put the Spanish translation for the second paragraph: it looks too long! It's only half a line longer but it looks denser. OK, we know that in Spanish you can read a little bit faster (you only need to watch the Spanish news on television to be made aware of that!). If you are confronted with a translation which looks like this one, alarm bells must start ringing. In this case it turned out that there were a couple more seconds left, but as a translator if you deliver that length you are in danger of having a very irate voice-over artist having to shorten the script live in the studio. Studio time and artist time are costly!!! Of course, it is not your fault, you did not have the time codes, you couldn't know! But…the client will be told in no uncertain terms by the narrator that the translation did not fit, that it is no good from his point of view. He is not interested in whether you did or did not have the time codes, or that you did not have a chance to watch the film. The client will know, but will he admit it? Very unlikely! He might be honest enough not to come back to tell you off, especially if you had warned him of the risks involved in doing a translation without the safety net of the time codes or the video.

You will also notice that the few notes about the script that are not going to be read are left in English, like (pause seven seconds). This sort of information (and sometimes you have more, giving you an indication of what scene is being shown, etc.) is extremely helpful to the sound engineer[3] and the editor when they put the film together with the voice; it helps them find their way through a script if they don't know the foreign language. So a script is more likely to look like this page with the "audio" column translated and the "visual" one remaining in the lingua franca, in other word the working language of the country you are in:

Audio	Visual
Das XXXX – Knochenmarkpunktionverfahren ist eine Modifikation der Standardpraxis der diagnostischen Knochenmark-punktierung. Ziel des Verfahrens ist etwa 30 bis 50 Milliliter Mark aus der hinteren Darmbeinkammregion für die Produktion von XXXX patientenspezifischen Gewebereparaturzellen zu gewinnen.	Scene 1: Quick dissolves of images from various points in the video, beginning with the arrival of the patient, a hand setting out the instruments, the patient being prepped and draped, an aspiration, and the aspirate being prepared for shipment to XXXXX. (pulls from final programme)
Am sichersten und leichtesten erhält man Mark vom hinteren Darmbeinkamm – genauer von der hinteren, oberen Darmbeinstachelregion.	Scene 2: Image of the posterior model; first, the entire crest is highlighted, then the spine region becomes highlighted. (Freeze of 01:15:07)
XXXXX Knochenmarkpunktionsverfahren basiert auf dem Konzept, so wenig Mark wie möglich von einer Stelle zu nehmen, und mehrere Stellen des Darm-beinkamms zu nutzen, was die Störung des Marks und das Absaugen peripheren Blutes minimiert. Wenn eine einzige Stelle mehrfach abgesaugt wird, wird das Mark in zunehmendem Maße gestört, was zu einer größeren Menge peripherem Blutes führt.	Scene 3: Graphic of the iliac crest, wipe to a close graphic of crest cross-section illustrating the seepage of peripheral blood into the marrow aspirate.

Table 6

Unless specifically asked by the client, do not translate the information that is not to be read. I know you might think that the more words you translate the more money you are going to make. If there are only a few of them, it will not make a big difference in the final invoice. You will do a "word count" on your computer and charge the full fee. However, if there are a lot of scene descriptions as in the example above, your clients might be a little bit surprised if you charge them for the total number of words. Having said that, many clients will ask for a quote before they give you the go-ahead or they will have counted the words themselves and it is for you to agree on the number then.

Here is an example of a translation in two columns.

Narrator: The first leg is 34 kilometres – even without the mist, this is a featureless stretch of desert with only the watering stations to show the riders how far they've travelled.	**Narrator**: Die erste Runde ist 34 Km lang. Auch ohne Nebel ist dies ein Stück konturlose Wüste, wo nur die Wasserstellen den Reitern zeigen, wie weit sie schon sind.
Narrator: The leaders complete the first loop in just over 90 minutes, returning to the village for the first vet check.	**Narrator**: Die Besten schaffen die 1. Runde in rund 90 Minuten und kommen zur Untersuchung durch den Tierarzt ins Dorf.
Narrator: In Endurance racing, the welfare of the horses is vital. <u>**The animals**</u> are checked after each stage and the teams work quickly to cool <u>**the horses**</u> and bring their heart rates down before they enter the vet stations.	**Narrator**: Beim Langstreckenrennen ist die Gesundheit der Pferde vorrangig. <u>**Sie**</u> werden nach jeder Runde untersucht. Die Teams kühlen <u>**sie**</u> und ihr Herzschlag wird heruntergebracht, bevor sie zum Tierarzt kommen.
Narrator: The vets check for soundness, quality of movement and skin lesions as well as measuring heart rates. They can disqualify an animal – or send it away to be re-presented if it's borderline, and that can cost valuable time.	**Narrator**: Der Arzt prüft den Gesundheitszustand, die Bewegungen, Hautverletzungen und den Herzschlag. Ein Pferd kann disqualifiziert werden oder, in Zweifelsfällen, später nachuntersucht werden, was wertvolle Zeit kosten kann.

Table 7

The time codes were not known. I have chosen a translation into German as we are always told: "Oh, German it is always much too long, it never fits!" Well you might not like the translation above for all sorts of reasons, but it works once it is put to picture with the proper voice and certainly you, as the translator, will know that it is going to fit the picture in terms of length. If you are picky you will see that the translator typed "Km" instead of the full word. Of course if that sort of thing was repeated often in the script it could affect the length quite considerably, but you can see here that even if the word had been typed in full it would not have made that much of a difference. You will notice a little trick used by the translator to shorten the script without cutting out any of the ideas. In the third paragraph for example, he replaced the words "The animals" and then "the horses" by "Sie" (=they). That is a typical way we go about keeping the length down. With some languages you can decide you will keep roughly the same number of words in your translation as in the original. That approach might work between some language pairs, but it is not always the case. If you look at paragraph three above, there are thirty-eight words in the original English and there are only twenty-eight in the translated German. If you used the word count method, that paragraph would be far too short… well yes, apart from the fact that German words are much longer as they are compounded words, so in general don't be tempted to use that method.

If you do not receive a script with time codes, you might receive a VHS with BITC, which stands for Burnt In Time Code.

It looks like the picture opposite. The BITC might be anywhere on the screen, generally at the top or the bottom. You use the top line to calculate your timings. The **10** in this case indicates the hours. It does not mean that the film is 10 hours long, it probably started on 10, but the editor could have started on 00 or 01. The next set of figures, **13**, are the minutes and it is the number of minutes you are into the film. **26** are the seconds. You should be concerned only with the minutes and the seconds really. The last set of figures, **15**, are the frame numbers, depending on the system. With PAL or Secam it could be 24 or 25 frames per second, and

there are other possibilities in digital filming, 29 or 30 frames for example, NTSC usually 29 or 29.97. Here we are talking about parts of seconds; therefore you should not concern yourself with frame numbers. The fastest way to get the time codes down is to print your script and have your finger on the pause button of your remote control. It is very unlikely that you can take down all the required time codes in the right place on the script if you do not pause. You will only write down the minutes and the seconds. You can then put them in your script like in my first example:

Duration in seconds
00:03:51:00 –
00:04:21:00
00:04:26:00 –
00:04:38:00
00:04:45:00 –
00:04:58:00
00:05:03:00 –
00:05:14:00

This client is very meticulous and had put the full time codes, which of course is useful for the editor as well; if you are writing the time codes down yourself, you only need the two figures in the middle, for example **03:51** and **04:21**. You can then work out that for this paragraph the voice will have **30** seconds to read it. Your script could then look something like this:

Table 8

19

Narrator	Duration in seconds
In the Middle East archaeologists have found traces from distillation devices, made of terracotta, dating as far back as 3500 BC. But they weren't necessarily used to refine alcohol though. Instead they often refined essential oils and rose water. Trying to bring out the purest and most refined ingredients. Al Kuhl. Later to be known as alcohol in Europe.	00:03:51:00 – 00:04:21:00 (30)
One of the first experiments with distillation in Europe is thought to have taken place at the Salerno School in Italy in the 12th century. Most of them behind closed doors.	00:04:26:00 – 00:04:38:00 (12)
Distillation was since long associated with alchemy and black magic. Some people even regarded the effects of the potion as supernatural.	00:04:45:00 – 00:04:58:00 (13)
A French Alchemist, Arnaud de Villeneuve, described it as "eau-de-vie – the elixir of eternal life".	00:05:03:00 – 00:05:14:00 (11)

Table 9

You will no doubt have noticed that I have added the number of seconds in brackets. This is very useful as you only have to calculate it once and you do not have to do the calculations again once your brain is really engaged in doing the translation and reading aloud to make sure it fits.

Well you might very well think, "Ok, now I understand all about time codes and length and I am confident I can rewrite the ideas rather than translating just the words." That should be easy enough with a bit of practice! Well, it gets tougher. What about when you have a series of words or statements that appear on the screen at the same time as you are speaking them. It makes for a very good and powerful presentation. If the spoken words appear too late or too early the original intended effect has gone and the foreign version will not be as good as the original and "we don't want that!" We want a **foreign** version which sounds as though it is an **original** version as well. This is another reason why it is very important, not to say vital, to have a copy of the film when you do your translation as it might very well be that there is no indication at all in the script about these 'bullet points".[4] There are no indications in the script about the writing on the screen because the client wants to save money and may/does not intend to have these words translated. Such onscreen-editing can be costly. (Changing the pictures on a film used to be prohibitive. However, with modern technology, the editing of a video is much easier, faster and cheaper, so there are more productions where each language version has got its own pictures, meaning some pictures can be frozen to add half a second here or there and indeed it has become possible to change the on-screen words into the appropriate language.)

We are therefore faced with the following scenarios: you have the words appearing on screen and the voice must fit exactly with them so that the viewers understand that they are hearing a translation of them; or the words have been translated on screen and you must make sure you know what they are in the target language if they have been translated before by someone else – for some reason this happens quite often. These words are buzz words used by the company, they already exist in a number of foreign languages for the company, but they might not tell you about them, so you need to ask for them. There is not much worse for the viewer than hearing one thing and reading something else in the same language. For example the word "contractor" in French can be translated in two different ways. It would therefore be unacceptable to have the word *maître d'oeuvre* on screen while the voice-over was reading the word *entrepreneur,* or vice versa. Instead of emphasising the point, it would distract the viewer who would try to work it out. By the way, when the client does not change the words on screen you will find it very difficult to convince the audience that they are watching a film that was made especially and only for them. However, whatever the language of the words on screen, you need to make sure that the spoken ones are going to fit as closely as possible to the ones appearing on screen. The same rule applies when you are describing in detail the working of a machine. The words must match the actions on the screen otherwise the mechanic might get really confused instead of learning the easy way to do this part of the job.

Here is an example from a translation we received where the words underlined and in bold had to fit to the same words appearing on screen:

English	Italian	Mandarin	Greek
Let your eyes adjust to the light. It's a vast land, full of contrasts. A land with over ten words for ice. Like **is stöpis, glasis, snöis...**	Dovete abituarvi alla luce di questa terra vasta, piena di contrasti e con più di dieci parole per ghiaccio come: **is, stöpis, glasis, snöis...**	讓眼睛適應光線。這片遼闊的土地，充滿了對比。在這裡代表冰的字眼有十幾個：如**is,stöp is, glasis, snöis...**	Αφήστε τα μάτια σας να προσαρμοστούν στο φώς. Είναι μια χώρα μεγάλη, γεμάτη αντιθέσεις. Μιά χώρα με πάνω από δέκα λέξεις για τον πάγο. Όπως **is, stöpis, glasis, snöis...**

Table 10

Well, it does not seem too bad if we go by the look of the columns. The Italian looks the best: there are even fewer words than in English. But really without the time codes it is impossible to know if it is going to fit or not. Also, in case you do not read Mandarin, each of the characters is a word and that sentence might be much longer to say than we might think when we look at it from the point of view of a non-Mandarin speaker. However, to me the Greek is worrying too. Let's see what happens when we double-check with the film, if we have got it in advance, or when we arrive at the studio and the voice-overs have to read it. Well I must say that Paolo, Deborah and Christina did a superb job. These translators have many years of practice in this sort of writing and I was delighted when it turned out that the words fitted extremely well to the pictures when the voices read them in the studio.

In this example the words for "ice" are not translated for two main reasons. First, they are probably not translatable in most languages, unless you are translating into other languages spoken by people in ice covered areas. And secondly, it is done on purpose to add some local colour to the script. In this instance the film-makers are proud of their product and its association with their country and therefore want to emphasise the fact that the viewers are watching a film which has been dubbed specifically into their own language. Ultimately it is trying to sell the product by associating it with the beauty and the charm of the country and its inhabitants.

Watching the film before you start the translation has a number of very big advantages. First, you become the viewer and you get acquainted with the story. You will see pictures that will automatically give you the right words, whereas the script might have been obscure, because the writer was playing on words. For example the word "spirit". Well, in a number of languages it means something relating to the soul **or** something you put in a glass! Now, the translator will probably know straight away when he sees the film, whether it is one or the other. However, if the writer is playing on the word and wants it to carry the two meanings, some translators will find it extremely difficult to translate into their own languages and will have to use the full context. To know the full context they will therefore need to have seen the film if they want to have half a chance of writing something meaningful, and yes indeed in the case of the word "spirit" something might be "lost in translation"! I know that is the case for this word in Greek and in Bulgarian, for example, as there is a word for "spirit = alcohol" and there is another one for "spirit = soul". So the translator needs to be totally immersed in the film and its mood to be able to recreate the "spirit" (sorry I could not resist using that word here, I could have said of course the "feeling" or the "atmosphere" of the film), without having the direct word for it.

That brings me to the second big advantage of watching the film. You will get the feeling of the film, you will get its atmosphere and that will help you in your translation. Some films are moodier than others. A film describing the working of a "combine harvester with axial flow" (that was the subject of the first film my company translated and voiced in 1982 into five languages) will not be as moody as one describing the making of whisky in Scotland for example. Not only the pictures but also the music will contribute to the atmosphere. The music is important for the feel it creates when you watch the film and therefore you have to listen carefully to what it does. You will notice when you translate the script that the original voice stops and there is nothing much happening for a few frames or even a couple of seconds. That might give you some breathing space to fit the few extra words you need for your sentence to be absolutely superb. However, beware, if the voice stops, there might very well be a reason for it. There could be a stomping big bang from the percussion department "fading up" – that is the technical expression for the music slowly coming up to a crescendo. If that is the case, you will not be able to use that time to put in your extra words. You must not only take account of the music but you also need to be aware of breaks in the script when a big noise happens. It could be a door closing or a hammer hitting a nail; all these things need to be taken into consideration when you do the translation. Now, having said all that, don't think it is an impossible task. The voice will also help, will know how to slow the delivery or accelerate it a little bit so that the explosion can be avoided or come closer to the "bullet-points" appearing on screen: this is what we call "fine tuning". But it is only "fine tuning". If the translation is way out, it will not work even with the best voice-over artist. I used the word "explosion" as an example because we have recently recorded a film where Alfred Nobel was mentioned. He invented dynamite to help the mining industry. When he realised what he had really done, he created the Nobel Peace Prize! In that film there was indeed a large explosion when speaking about Nobel's discovery.

The length is therefore one of the most important aspects of translating for voice-overs. Some languages need fewer words than others to express the same idea, and of course to translate into these languages is relatively easier than when it is the other way around. I am always on the look out for articles and information about languages, and I recently came across an article[5] about a language called Nootka. The research had been undertaken by a team from Newcastle about this tongue spoken by North American tribes in the Rockies. It has been spoken for 5,000 years; it uses an alphabet made up of forty consonants and three basic vowels, which means that the sound structure is very complex, according to researcher John Stonham of Newcastle University. He started studying this language twenty years ago. He has now published a dictionary containing 150,000 words. However, what is of interest to us is that Nootka has the peculiarity of being very concise. One of the examples given is quite amazing. "To wipe the tears from one's eye with the back of one's hand" is translated by: "fib". How easy it would be if the language you had to translate into was like that. Mind you it would be a headache to translate from that language. Before you feel too enthusiastic about learning Nootka and starting to write voice-overs in that language, I feel I should also inform you that there are only 300 people left who speak it and they are almost all over sixty!!!

The length, the atmosphere, the feeling, all these factors are important if you want to make a good translation, so in the absence of a film you have to use all the tricks I mentioned before. You must also try to have a little chat with the film director or the writer or someone who has seen the film, so that they can describe to you in as much detail as possible what type of production it is you are translating. With experience acquired through the years you will know, or rather you will guess, what is going on on-screen. In fact it is not unusual for me to see the film in my head while translating, even if I have not seen the real thing, but it takes a few years to acquire this feeling for the type of translation you are confronted with. I suppose it is a bit quicker to acquire this experience nowadays as clients find it easier to send the films to the translators. In the early days the voices who were translators themselves acquired the experience in the studio by dubbing the films themselves. When I first started, clients very often insisted on the translator being able to voice as well. At the time translators who had no experience in voicing and who were never presented with a copy of the film to do the translation could not imagine what was going on on-screen and produced on the whole pretty bad translations, in our terms.

The readability

And we now come to the readability. It is very important to remember that the viewer is only going to watch the film once. In the world of industry and commerce the employees do not have much time for training. Even in very good companies where training is offered by the top management, managers in the field have targets to meet and do not like to waste time on their staff watching fancy videos made by HQ! So if you are lucky enough for your script to be heard by the intended audience it is very unlikely that they will have the time to listen to it more than once. With that in mind you must try to be as clear as possible. In my experience, translations have very often been clearer than the original English. Sometimes your queries might even lead the client to revise, and re-edit the original English! You must not be shy of asking clients for clarification on the usage of words or sentences. If it is not clear to you in the first place, you cannot write a clear script. And you can't put notes at the bottom of the page to explain things either! I have often heard the expression in the translating world "garbage in–garbage out". Well I disagree with that approach. I will always try to explain the situation as tactfully as possible to the client or to the original writer. I will play on the fact that I am a foreigner and that I need an explanation. Well, admittedly, sometimes it is exactly that; even after thirty years in the business, there are things a translator might not be familiar with and he or she will discover a new field and learn some new words, new expressions, and even new syntax all the time.

So, do not hesitate to go back to the client to ask for clarification of sentences. The client or the writer will sometimes recognise that the sentence does not make much sense and rewrite it or give you guidance on what was really intended by it. Don't take a guess, just ask, sometimes it is a spelling mistake or the punctuation that need to be rectified. A comma might suddenly make everything clearer. I can hear your thought, yes, I know, sometimes you will be able to work it out for yourself. Another point to take into consideration is that you do not want to antagonise your client or the writer, so as I mentioned before,[6] diplomacy is important in your approach.

However, there is also another factor that you need to remember. Do not jump on the phone at the first difficulty. Make a clear list of all the points where you feel you need to know more and then contact the client. In my experience, I don't think they will mind that, but if you were to contact them every five minutes that would become a burden to them. They have other fish to fry and they thought that you as the translator were going to deal with all the problems, not harass them with one question after another. I know about that, because I do use translators myself and feel a little bit annoyed if the queries are not grouped together in a clear e-mail. You might have had a similar experience as a translator; there is nothing more disturbing than a client coming back to you with late changes once you have almost finished the translation, so that you need to go back through the entire translation to check what sort of effects these changes will have on the full script. Or, even worse, the client decides on a preferred choice of words once the translation has been completed. I have had a recent case of this when the client decided the word "contractor" should be translated in the entire 20,000-word document as *entrepreneur,* which is a good translation of the word. But as we have already seen, this word can legitimately be translated in two different ways. However, the translator had gone for *Maître d'oeuvre*; that worked very well because there was also the expression "works contractor", *which* had been translated as…*entrepreneur;* so we now had to use *entrepreneur de travaux.* It is completely irrelevant that I preferred the original as *the client is always right!* The full text, with hundreds of occurrences of these words, had to be revised. So please remember to make one list and try to make it as easy for your clients as you wish they would make it for you. By the way, in that case, the client being very good and understanding language matters well, there was an additional fee for the late changes! But that is not often the case, far from it.

There are also countless occasions when the original is badly written and your questioning will lead to an improved original and a good foreign version. You must not forget that the judge is not really your client or the writer of the original script. The real judge is going to be the audience, the mechanic learning to change a part in a brand new engine for a car which has been recalled or the surgeon trying a new approach to repair a damaged valve in a human heart! The audience doesn't want to think that they are listening to a dubbing. To them it is the film that matters and the fact that it might have been made in Japan, Britain or Timbuktu is totally irrelevant! (By the way I actually lived near Timbuktu in Mali as a child; it was next door really in African terms, only about a thousand kilometres away!)

So clarity is of the essence because the message must be understood first time around. A good test for that is to read it aloud. If you find it difficult to read or if you fluff all or some of the words, you know that there is something wrong. OK, you know that the professional reader is going to find it easier to read than you, but if you can't read your own prose aloud, then there are, without any doubt, a number of problems to be rectified. It is better to make two short sentences rather than a very long one;

we are not all Proust and anyway he did not write to be recorded! You must be thinking by now: "What is he talking about; he rambles on and on and makes long sentences and detours?" Well, you see, it is very easy to do that, to go astray and to come back. It is, I suppose, the nature of storytelling. It is easy and it can work when it is on paper, because you use commas and semi colons and brackets, and it works as well when you talk in front of a live audience because you add your body language and your own personality, but it does not work when you are a voice-over, a disembodied voice, an anonymous voice. So the message must be clear and to the point. Forget your law degree or your desire to write speeches for politicians, a good voice-over script is the antithesis of that type of spin writing!

Let me quote here from the play *Brontë* by Polly Teale which was performed at the Lyric Theatre in November 2005. This is Heger telling the Brontë sisters how to write: "You must all choose your words as you would choose a weapon, that it may do precisely as you intend. Economy, Restraint, Sacrifice everything that does not contribute to clarity. Only when you have control, purpose, precision. Only then can you let the reins fly." Look at this short speech: not only the message is clear, but it is also a perfect example of what the spoken word should be. Try it and see how easy it is to read aloud.

You will need to try to keep the impact some of the words have in the original. Some sentences will end with a bang, which is not always retained in the translation where the words sort of fizzle out. If it is at all possible in your language you must keep the enthusiasm. Very often in corporate videos the end of the production or of some sections are very strong, requiring something called a **hard** sell type of delivery. Some other scripts are more subtle and you will need a **soft** sell type. You must try to keep these styles of delivery in your translations otherwise the voice will find it extremely difficult to sound right. I know that to a foreign ear, Finnish, to take just one example, does not sound very enthusiastic, but I am sure the Finns have ways of expressing enthusiasm and that is what the translators should try to achieve in their scripts. Emotions are not translated in the same way in every language and we have to cope with that. I would like to emphasise the importance of "interpreting" your translation to make sure it is a good one for the purpose of a voice-over. If you want to read all about the debate on the different types of translations and interpretations, I thoroughly recommend Umberto Eco's *Mouse or Rat?* This book was first published in 2003. He goes into detail and with great methodology into the different types of translations; some of his explanations concerning the translation of poems is quite relevant to our own field of translating the spoken word. He puts great emphasis on the importance of rhythm which is also part of what we need to do to produce a good voice-over script.

By now, if you are still with me, you will know most of what is required to start translating the spoken word and therefore diversify your work (which is always stimulating when you tend to work on your own in your office, sitting at your computer). You might have been translating the same sort of material for quite a few years and a new departure into translating for voice-overs would probably be very challenging. Yes, it is a challenge and if you have what it takes to do it, you will enjoy it thoroughly; it will give you the opportunity to meet new people in a different working environment. Writing for voice-over is not the end of the road for your newly acquired style of writing. You will find numerous other opportunities to translate the spoken word. With the new media all around us there are also new markets, new applications that create new needs for translations. One example of this is the booming market in telephone prompts. There are of course the simple ones that everybody is familiar with, you know the sort that gets up your nose because, really, you would like to speak to somebody and not to have to press one of the eight or nine options and then to listen to another five, and to another three, and then wait for an operator to be free. These have to be translated as well of course, but there are also many companies which used to send paper questionnaires to be filled in by ticking boxes but are nowadays replacing what they consider an archaic method by something more modern. They let the respondents "fill in" the questionnaires over the phone. The company is presented by a warm voice, very often a woman's voice, and then the questions are asked and the listener only needs to press one of the keys on the telephone to give the answer. (I would like to give a little note to translators who might have had a problem, or who might have it in the future, with a word used in the United States. The expression is "Press the Pound key". Well, we translate from English and not from American so some translators got caught by this word. They only saw the word and forgot the context, so they translated it as the word for the Pound Sterling. It is not the "£" for the simple reason that this does not appear on a telephone. Mind you, the translator might never have been to the USA and thought, well, "Why not, they must have slightly different signs on their telephones there!" It would have been well worth asking the client what was exactly meant rather than sending back words like press "*esterlinas*"! (It was not only the Spanish translator who got it wrong…)

Anyway to cut a long story short what the Americans call the "Pound key" is this one, "#", referred to as the "hash key" most of the time in English, also sometimes the "number key". If you are old enough you will remember that at the greengrocer when you bought your vegetables the sign for a pound in weight of say potatoes was "#": this is why our American cousins call it the Pound key.)

Some very serious work is being done this way and in the long term it saves the companies a lot of money. For example, large pharmaceutical companies do some of their research like this. They only need to send a freephone number to the doctors, nurses and/ or patients who can then reply to the survey over the phone rather than by filling in a bulky document. They do not have to spend thousands on printing and postage and on handling all those letters. The handling of the questionnaires when they are returned is also simplified as the results given on the phone are collated and analysed by a computer.

Another area of translation which requires the spoken word rather than the written one is on-board announcements for airline companies. This has also increased tremendously in the past few years for two major reasons. One is the larger number of airline companies and passengers and the other is that by law safety announcements must be available on all aircraft in the languages of the people being carried. One political event which has had a great impact in this area is the fall of the Berlin Wall, and the lifting of the Iron Curtain. With the demise of the USSR, many of the republics have become independent or autonomous and as such have reverted to their own language as the official language of the country. They might not have abandoned Russian altogether since it is quite useful as the common language of communication throughout the ex-empire. Russian was the *lingua franca* for about seventy years in the East European republics and before that, the Russia of the Tsars had expanded East and South to cover very large territories where Russian was also the main language. Russian has been superseded in many places and there are now dozens of "new" languages, and that can only be a bonus for translators and voices. Until 1990, who would have bothered to translate anything (I am not talking about literature) into Georgian or Ukrainian for example? With the dislocation of Yugoslavia, we now have to translate and record into Serb and Croatian rather than in Serbo-Croatian as was the case as long as Tito kept the different republics unified. A similar thing has happened with Czechoslovakia. We now do two versions: one into Czech and one into Slovak. Again very good news for linguists!

The market and the opportunities for translators and voices are expanding as the need for verbal communication increases all the time all over the world.

1 I heard this expression in a production of *Wind In The Willows* and liked it so much that I could not resist using it here.

2 FTP stands for File Transfer Protocol, not for Franc-Tireurs et Partisans as French speakers might have thought. I mentioned them in another book!

3 The sound engineer is also called the Studio Manager and at the BBC this is often shortened to SM.

4 I love this expression; it makes me think I am in an action film!

5 *Guardian* article published on 31st May 2005.

6 Use of "before" spoken language for "above" written language, I am sure you will spot hundreds of similar examples in this work.

SPEAKERS
IN VISION

"Down and under"

The next step in your career as a translator of the spoken word is to start writing scripts for people who are speaking in vision. We will take the example of the managing director of a multinational. There are more of these types of companies than one might think: to be a multinational you only need to have a few operations going on in a few countries. The managing director wants to be close to the workforce overseas but, at the same time, he does not want to travel the world all the time to see them. Travel is time-consuming and expensive. When he does travel, he wants to meet the big boys and sign lucrative contracts. So, one way to keep in touch is via a television address. It could be done live via satellite, or recorded and sent on DVD, or be uploaded to an Internet site. The medium is not really relevant to the work translators will have to do. In the case of a live transmission a translator will not be required; it will be the work of an interpreter (or many interpreters, as the case may be). The managing director is speaking to the workforce in his own language, or maybe in English. The viewers know that. They readily accept the fact that the managing director is not going to be able to speak to everyone in the corporation in their own language. (Mind you, the previous Pope, John Paul 2nd, was not bad at languages! He was trying to address his flock all over the world in their own language and seemed to be doing a very good job of it! Though far be it from me to compare him to an MD –

and I mean managing director here, not Mini Disk!) Therefore there will not be any attempt at pretending otherwise. The voice-over in this case will be a little different from a narration. It will still be the spoken word; length and timing will still be problematic.

For this sort of production, the voice of the MD will be heard for a second or two, right at the beginning then faded under the voice of the artist speaking in his own language. This "down and under" mixing will be done by the studio engineer; he will dip the voice of the MD under the voice of the artist. (When you do that sort of thing with music the studio manager might use the expression "duck the music".) However, the translator and the voice will have to help him. In such a situation it is always better to have a translation slightly shorter than the original as this allows for the voice of the MD to be heard in between. A few words at the beginning and at the end of each paragraph will make the message more personal which is the aim of the production in the first place. Now, you might also be able to give life to the production by looking at the body language of the MD and whenever possible give the voice the opportunity of putting the right words in the right place. It is not always possible and it is not always expected, but if it happens a few times in the presentation it makes it look much better and livelier than if it cannot be achieved. These are the little things that make the difference between acceptable translations and dubbing and good ones.

Another advantage of watching the film is that sometimes you will notice that the MD is not constantly in vision. There might be pictures illustrating what he is talking about, graphics and so on. That will help, in so far as if you don't see him, you don't have to worry about the body language, and it is also easier to cut some words out. Another reason why it is wise to see the "man" in action is that people speak or read at different speeds. (I am aware I have been using the word "man" when it could have been "woman". It only reflects, I suppose, the harsh reality of the business world. Most MDs are men, but if it is a woman, the same rules apply to the translations!) Don't forget, the MD might not be a professional presenter, even though he might have had some coaching in this area to get that sort of job. Some will be adlibbing and speaking very fast because they keep repeating the same things all day long, some will have had the script prepared by a specialist and will read it from an "autoprompt" also known as an "autocue". Some skill is required for reading from a prompt and you also need to have a professional prompt operator or else you might find that the one cannot follow the other and that the delivery will be going either slower and slower or faster and faster. MD speeches are not always perfect in terms of delivery (I would not presume to comment on the content!), and might indeed become better in the foreign versions when they are read by professional voices. Having said all that, it is very difficult, although necessary, to consider all these factors when you do your translation.

You will not always have to translate MD speeches. You will find that in some films there is a narrator who is off-screen, but that there are other people appearing on-screen to say a few lines. Particular attention will have to be paid to the translation of these "vox pops" as we call them. Indeed, if you have a fifteen-second long paragraph off vision, the voice can probably gain one or two seconds to make the paragraph fit without sounding ridiculously fast. However, if the sentence spoken is only three seconds long or shorter, the translation must be extremely succinct as there won't be much the voice can do to help. For all the reasons I have alluded to earlier it is also important to ascertain if the vox pop is a man or a woman. Sound bites are very difficult to translate for dubbing purposes. With very short sentences on screen, there will probably be no time to hear the original voice at the beginning or the end. It will probably be kept at a very low level under the voice-over. Not too long ago I saw a very nice programme on ARTE – the Franco-German television station based in Strasbourg, which broadcasts its programmes both in French and in German. Many of the programmes are originally in French or in German and are dubbed for the other country. I was watching a documentary on the Provence region of France on the German-speaking channel of ARTE and I realised that the voice-over had been done superbly.

The interviews and the original narration in French had been written and cut in such a way that the interviews could be heard both in the French original and in the German translation. There was enough space in between sentences or paragraphs to have the German translation. One might think the programme would be too long and boring, but it wasn't, thanks to the quality of the editing and the beauty of the pictures. That is the sort of thing that can be achieved when film directors know there will be different language versions and when they are also aware of the problems faced by the translators. In the case of ARTE, I expect the translators are more writers than translators and are able to work on the project from the start. I would be glad of any comments on that.

"Phrase-synch"

The synchronisation of phrases, known as "phrase-synch" is the cheap version of the "lip-synch" done for feature films. For corporate videos, or should I say for corporate DVDs nowadays, there is rarely a budget to do a full lip synchronisation. Clients therefore go for "phrase-synch". This is done mainly for training productions when we have to dub people doing role plays. There will be a number of scenes trying to illustrate the dos and the don'ts of selling, for example. A lot of material is produced to train sales people. It is quite understandable that they are the part of the workforce on which most attention will be lavished, as they are ultimately the ones who bring in the money for the company to stay in business. Admittedly, the production side also needs to be well trained as the sales people could not work if they did not have anything to sell! Phrase-synch is a challenge for the translator of the spoken word. In this case you have to deal with each sentence on its own: each one needs to fit. What we are trying to achieve is a sound coming out of the mouth of the speaker when the mouth is open and silence when he is not speaking. Add to that another constraint given to you by the writer of the original script. There are key words, key sentences that need to be translated in an approved way in the industry concerned. The message is more important than the look on the screen but you still don't want to have sounds coming out of a closed mouth and vice versa if you can avoid it! The rule of thumb to achieve this effect is not so much the timing, even though that is useful and necessary. The main factor you need to use is the number of syllables in the sentence. If you can achieve the same number of syllables, you are going to produce a script which is going to fit. You can of course perfect that by looking at the way the sentence ends. If for example the last syllable in the sentence sounds like "it" but in your language it is "to", it will not be such a wonderful phrase synch, though it is OK if there is no other way. Try it by saying these two syllables aloud and looking at your lips in a mirror and you will realise straight away that it is not going to look very good. You might not be able to find a syllable that will produce the same shape of the mouth at the end of the sentence, but if you can achieve that sometimes, well your translation will help improve the end product.

You can also improve on that by looking inside the sentence. Where the speaker breathes, the mouth might be open with no sound coming out, only air coming in. If your sentence can be structured in such a way that the voice will be able to breathe in the same space, here again you will gain some brownie points. This sort of training production tends to be long – thirty or fifty minutes or more – and you might have a number of episodes to translate. But don't be frightened – there is still hope! When looking at the film carefully you will notice that some of the characters are turned away from the camera, or are far away, so these scenes are going to be relatively easy. You might even get a bonus when you discover that the actors are still talking but pictures cover them to show some manuals or graphics or anything else the director thinks is important to show the student. It could be the material they will have to use when they make a sales call or the forms they will have to fill in when they get back to the office. That gives us a bit of breathing space. Look out for anything that hides the mouth movements. And never forget to speak your own words aloud, all the time, just to make sure. Well at least for the first twenty years! (I am a slow learner!)

"Lip-synch"

From here the logical step is to go on to full lip synchronisation for feature films. However, this is highly specialised. There is almost no tradition of this in Great Britain as foreign films tend to be subtitled. However, on the European continent there is a thriving industry in Paris, Munich, Rome and Madrid as well as a few lesser known centres. It is the work more of a writer than a translator and I will not be able to tell you much about this as I have never actually written lip-synch though as an actor I have had to do it a few times. Here again it is a niche for a few specialists who do it all the time. If you have seen dubbed films, you might have remarked that very often, especially on television, the voices all sound the same. It is partly because very often they are the same, but also because of the nature of the recording techniques which forces the actors to work in a similar manner and does not allow them always to do what they would like with their voices; there are so many constraints. In the UK the actors work from a script and are helped by Electronic Wipes: two fixed vertical lines on each side of the screen, with a third one that wipes across it and when it reaches the vertical line on the right it is time to start speaking. Sometimes you are also helped by the Countdown Bleeps; three bleeps are played in the cans to give you a warning and you start speaking on the fourth bleep. These are the two most commonly used methods in the UK. It is not ideal.

On the continent the lines of script are written by hand on a sort of "ticker tape", known as *la bande rythmo* in French (called the *Bande* system, pronounced as Band, in English), which moves under the screen. In studios used for this type of synchronisation, the screens are very large so that the actors and the director can have a very good look at the lips. I said the script is written by hand because the writer will be able to indicate with his or her calligraphy the length of a vowel for example, so a long sounding "o" will look like a rugby ball! I said this work is done by a writer as the words might be completely different in meaning from the original, just to make sure that the lips move the right way. But at the same time the story must be told in such a way that a romance must not become a drama or a war film a fantasy. I remember a number of television productions in the '70s and the '80s that the British tried to lip-synch instead of subtitling. For example, there was a Chinese series called *The Water Margins* where the lip movements were completely out of synch and when a French soap, *Château Vallon*, was dubbed it did not fare much better and was a flop. As I mentioned earlier, some language pairs are easier to translate than others, but still, specialists can do a pretty good job at lip-synching. The one aspect I don't like about lip-synched films, and I am talking here about technical aspects, not trying to put a value judgement on this technique, is the lack of attention to detail taken in the actual recordings. In Great Britain, when television films are made, great care is taken over the sound atmosphere. For example if a scene is happening in a bathroom, it sounds as though it is in a bathroom. If the scene is shot outside in a busy Spanish street, there will be some "rhubarb" ("rhubarb" is a jargon word used when actors are making sounds which don't make any sense but which are supposed to recreate the sound of a crowd), so, when some "rhubarb" is being recorded, some real Spaniards are also recorded speaking or shouting in their own tongue so that the atmosphere becomes completely right. This is something our continental neighbours don't seem to care about. To me, American series, or for that matter any other television series, dubbed into French, German, Italian or Spanish, all sound as though they have been recorded in a bathroom!

With the advent of satellite television it is now possible to zap through hundred of channels and watch films or programmes in many different languages. No doubt there are interesting things to discover in the way other television stations do things differently from the one I watch from time to time. One which always makes me smile is the way Poland has been dubbing films. It is not that I understand the language, even though I am quite familiar with it as I live in an area of London where there are many Poles and I also direct or record Polish voices quite often. In Poland, films are dubbed in such a way that you do not actually really need to understand Polish. They do not attempt to record a lip-synch at all. There is a single voice saying what all the actors are saying on screen and the original sound track in the background is quite loud so you can actually watch the film and understand what is going on without too much difficulty. It is especially easy with action films, where there is not much said anyway!

For feature films, things are different and great attention is generally given to making a good job of it, to such an extent that people think it has been shot in their own language. This process is known as ADR (Automatic Dialogue Replacement). Mind you, there is nothing much automatic about it according to some studio engineers. In the United States they still use the expression "looping" to describe this type of work, which comes from the times when films were cut into loops, so that the scene could be seen again and again and the recordings made until the dubbing was to the satisfaction of the director. In the old days of cinema, in the '30s when "silent movies" became "talkies", if a film was going to be shown in more than one language it had to be shot from the start in the different languages. Admittedly this meant that the film was going to cost much more as it would take longer to shoot and edit. The example I have in mind are the six or seven films in which Maurice Chevalier was starring which were shot both in American and French. I don't know if you have seen any of Maurice Chevalier's films in English, but he had a very strong and typical French accent when he performed. His accent has become the archetype of the French accent. There is the anecdote about him asking the film director: "Ise dère ineuf accent?" Many Americans on the set smiled, to say the least, when they heard him ask that question. There was no other way to have two versions then.

Nowadays there is a very interesting practice in co-productions. Films are very expensive to make so it happens more and more often that a number of countries get together to make a film. Of course they all want to have their household names in the film. You may therefore have a famous French actress who will have as her partner a perfect English gentleman, and the villain will no doubt be played by a German and so on. The interesting thing about all this is that quite often the actors are all speaking in their own language. The advantage of that is that in the dubbing, say for the French audience, a number of actors will actually be speaking French and will not be dubbed and the same thing happens of course for the other languages with the other actors. On the down side, it makes acting even more challenging for the performers as they might have difficulties understanding the actor in front of them. However, in real life, they all have a script they can understand and even if they cannot understand the actual words they know the feeling that is being expressed by their partner and it seems to work pretty well, without the public realising that it is happening.

Very often the actors go back to the studio to dub themselves for scenes which have been shot outdoors so that the sound is perfect. When recording on location, all sorts of things can happen, like a church bell tolling every fifteen minutes. It actually happened while I was on a shoot recently playing the part of a French Mayor in *The Flying Scotsman*.[1] As this production was financed partly by German money as well as Scottish funds, the French village had to be in Germany. It looked pretty convincing once the decorators had put up French and Scottish flags everywhere, but the bells were there relentlessly every fifteen minutes. I think we managed to do all the shots in between, but it might very well have been that some of us could be recalled to do some of the lines. This type of speech replacement is relatively easy as the right words have been said in the first place. OK, OK, I am going off subject a bit here. Let's get back to translation.

So, translating for lip-synch is really an art and if you are very interested in films, you might very well want to start working on it. The training will be hard, but who knows you might discover that you are the one who can do it. Like all arts some will have it in them and will be able to express it, some others will not have it and try unsuccessfully for ever, and some will never be discovered. So the only way to find out, like in everything else in life, is to have a go at it! If you cannot find a university course to learn how to do it, you might want to try to work on your phrase synch and try to achieve lip-synch as often as you can. It will take you longer to do your translation, but you would be acquiring a new skill. This would be quite a good way to find out if this is something you can do. You might discover that you like the challenge and work hard at training yourself. At the same time you would be giving your client a better than expected translation which is never a bad thing. Once you are confident you can do it well you can then advertise yourself and start doing it for good and charge accordingly…

---

1   Graeme Obree beat the Hour World Record on a bicycle in 1993 on the Olympic track in Hamar, Norway and again the following year in Bordeaux, France. He is the subject of that film.

THE CREATIVITY

As you progress in the field of translating for voice-overs you will want to use your creativity more and more. I am talking here about doing more than what I said earlier when I told you to ask the client for freedom of interpretation. What I am talking about here is getting involved in the process earlier when the client is writing the original concept. Some input from the translators at this point can be extremely useful to the client and the end-product and will make your life easier when the time comes to do the translation. Some clients have from time to time asked my advice about a future project. They wanted to know, for example, if a sentence or a title will be translatable in a number of languages and they knew already which languages they would require. It is then for me to let them know. I might already know the answer for some of the languages or I might have to find out from the translators.

Some little help like that to clients will probably not be charged at this stage, the clients are not asking for the translations just yet, they only want to know if it will be translatable and if the concept will be easily understood in the different languages.

I remember an advertising campaign, years ago, I am not sure about the product, it is irrelevant anyway. The pictures were going to show a happy family using a four-by-four in a stunning landscape and to complete the family they had this beautiful Golden Labrador. Millions were spent on making the commercial and it was never shown to its original market, simply because the intended market was in the Arab world where dogs are considered impure in the Koran. Flop! Waste of money!

Why did they not acquire a bit of local knowledge? I am almost certain an Arabic translator would have told them straight from the start that it was a no-goer!

So offering your client your knowledge at the start of the production could lead to a long-standing relationship between the two of you. Your input might become more and more appreciated and you might find yourself starting to write scripts for your clients, or parts of scripts instead of translating them. You might in fact be learning a new job; you will stop translating what someone else wrote, you will write yourself! Of course, you might tell me, but that is not my job, I don't want to write. Fair enough, but if you have read so far, it probably means you like a new challenge. In that case, yes, you will need to develop new skills, you will have to learn to take a brief, and become acquainted with the subject matter. You might start to know the field so well that after a few years you might even feel that you are part of that company. It might even turn out that you will retain knowledge about a specific company that nobody else has. Members of staff move on, are replaced, translation departments in many of the largest companies have closed. Multinationals knew the importance of having a team of translators with inside knowledge and access to internal resources that outsiders do not have, but at one stage these managers were replaced by accountants who thought a translation department was far too costly, and that it would be much better to outsource. The beauty of that is that you only pay for the work which is actually done, you do not have to pay for pensions, or when people are sick.

This is of course a very short-term view of the situation; it does not take into account what translating really means. All the knowledge accumulated in the department disappears. I have actually lived through that sort of situation with a very large company, and I mean very large. The translation bureau was almost closed with just a couple of people left to order the translations from an outside agency. I don't know exactly what happened and what the reasons were, but in the last few months it seems that the office is being enlarged again and that I am asked to translate for them once more! I have another example of the relationship that you can build with a company, again quite a large multinational. I first started doing translation and voice work for that company when they started their operation in France in 1986. I have voiced all their training material and it is a company strong on training, not only for the salesmen but also for the technical staff as the work is very delicate and needs to achieve the highest standards to be successful. I have gone on Roadshows with them in France and in French-speaking Belgium. I have organised workshops on presentation techniques to some of their managers. Since 1986 they have probably had about a dozen managing directors, but I am still working for them. So in a way I have more of an overview of what that company has been doing than almost anyone else.

And when it comes to translating or writing I have the background knowledge that is normally associated with an in-house translation department. So, as I was saying earlier, opening the door to translating for the spoken word might lead to unexpected professional experiences. I remember once being sent around a number of steel manufacturing plants in France to find out ways of saving them! In the late '70s and early '80s after a couple of crippling hikes in the price of a barrel[1] of petrol, heavy industries were having a very hard time. The steel industry was very badly affected by the prevailing deterioration of the economy and most of the steel plants in the West did not survive. But what an experience for someone used to sitting behind a typewriter to have to go on site, take notes, ask questions, work with a team of specialists and produce a document at the end! Admittedly, having worked in a newsroom was a useful skill for that sort of work, but translating other people's work also tremendously helped in that case. Translating had given me not only a wide general knowledge but also the feel for the sort of style required. I don't know if you have ever been in a steel manufacturing plant, but it is awe-inspiring, the sheer size of it, the molten steel running like lava on the slope of a volcano. It reminded me of Dante's *Inferno* and of William Blake's illustrations, but the Devil had nothing to do with it, it was all manmade!

1   You might like to know that a barrel contains 159 litres of petrol, so
     when there is an increase of 10 dollars to a barrel which is considered a
     hefty increase, it is only about 6 cents per litre!

THE NEWSROOM
SYNDROME

I have alluded to this point about speed of turnaround earlier, but I would like to emphasise its importance. It is the nature of our 24/24 society that things must be done quickly. Deadlines are very important for clients. As suppliers of services to clients in the global village we have to go along with that. Our specialist niche is part of the media, maybe not the glamorous part of TV shows or even television news but we are still part of this culture. Sometimes we are very close to it, as in the case of the managing director delivering a speech about a company's affairs. His speech might have an impact on the financial markets of the world. The local managers need to know about it as soon as the chairperson has finished talking so as to be able to respond accordingly in the local markets. This is when a very fast turn around is required. In other cases the presentation will need to be ready in the foreign languages for an international exhibition which is going to happen on a given date and there cannot be any delay, your work cannot be late. However, I hear you screaming the way I have done many times! They have known about this show for a year, or even longer, it happens every year at the same time, why did they not plan it in time? Well, some clients learn, some don't!

There is one valid excuse, up to a point, and it is when, for example, the last quarterly figures will be given officially during that broadcast. But even then a lot of the work could have been prepared beforehand, leaving 'XXX' where the figures will need to be entered. It would only take a few minutes to finalise the script, it could even be phoned in to the studio while the voice gets ready to record the programme and some of my clients have done that very well in the past. Some! There are other reasons why the translation is left to the last minute. A large company just manages to secure a meeting with a potential client and they would like to impress them with a presentation in their own language. The large manufacturer knows that some of the people they are going to meet speak English, but what an impact on the entire climate of the meeting if they could present their company, say in Catalan. I am choosing this example as we were involved in a very successful operation in the early '80s using this language. The Catalans were once more becoming the power-house of Spain and at the same time wanted not only to preserve their language and own culture as distinctive from the Spanish one, but also to promote it.

Our client, dare I say, an American Corporation, was very much aware of the socio-cultural happenings in that autonomous region of Spain and had the brilliant idea of making a version in Catalan. There was not much time for the turnaround as you might guess. The client arrived with his video, managed to greet the Catalans with a few words of Spanish and then went on in English. After the first few minutes he realised that half the audience did not understand what he was saying, so he told them in a few words that he had brought them a video to introduce his Corporation. They just could not believe it, the "imperialist" had made them a video in their own language, not in English, not in Spanish, no, in Catalan, therefore recognizing them as a fully-fledged people, in other words, showing respect! The effect was so strong that the competition did not have a chance and this Corporation won the contract! Imagine the difference, if the translators had not been able to deliver in time and the video had been shown in English! The Catalans being more secure now, the impact would probably not be as striking in Barcelona today and would not necessarily guarantee a sale, but it did then!

There are also very bad excuses for the lateness of a project. The foreign language versions are an afterthought. "Why not make foreign versions?" The client has spent a lot of money making a beautiful film; mind you, you might disagree on the quality of the production, but that is another question we won't go into. So, the clients have spent a lot of money, and they think yes, let's get it translated, it can't cost much, all the work has already been done! These are the worst clients: they have never done it before, they haven't got a clue about foreign languages, and the learning curve will be painful for you and maybe for them. So proud of their film are they that they ask the production company to give them an estimate to translate the film into the twenty-five languages spoken in all the territories where they have some operations going on. The production company will have experience of foreign languages or maybe not, and will enquire to find out about costs. They might come to our company or to some of the others in the field – there are not that many that provide both translations and voice-overs by professional translators/writers and voices. We will tell them what the cost is going to be, the production company will add their cost and they will pass it on. The client, if he is standing is going to fall down or sag in his chair if he is sitting, and disappear under his desk! That is far too expensive, we cannot do that, they have no idea that language specialists are expensive, they do not flinch at the costs of their accountants, solicitors or lawyers, but they don't know that linguists are "professionals" as well.

How can we reduce the cost? Well, there are a number of ways, the most sensible one, if you know how much you can spend, is to reduce the number of languages and only do the ones where the largest possible audience will watch the film. The other countries, like for example the Scandinavian ones and the Netherlands, will have to do with the English version – after all, they are used to watching films in original versions in these countries. So they decide to do five foreign versions instead of twenty-five. So far so good, they are prepared to pay the fee to have their five versions done professionally and they have not wasted too much time in coming to that decision, but the delay has been reduced a bit and once more the translators will have to make up the time. However, there are other companies where they want their five versions, but they still want to save money, so they hit on the brilliant idea that the scripts should be translated in-house. Not that they have a translation bureau at headquarters that would be reasonably qualified to do that sort of work, oh no, they are going to ask people they know in the different countries to do it for nothing. They will not take into consideration the fact that these people have got jobs that require all their time, no, they will just have to squeeze that in. Or even better, the sister of the MD is married to a French guy who is going to do it for little money, he has been in this country for thirty years and he speaks English very well so he will be able to translate it without any problems at all! He does not know anything about the company and he has not written an essay since he left school! This approach is like playing Russian roulette with only one empty space in the magazine! Most of the time the results will be a disaster! The translation will be delivered late because the people asked to do it in the company have too much on their plate as it is. They cannot see why they should be asked to do something which is not part of the job description. They also delay doing it because they feel they will not be able to do it and it will take them a very long time, but they are put under such pressure that they finally do it at the last minute, in a hurry. The translation will be badly written, in the best cases it will be in the wrong style, written for publication in a brochure or a manual and of course it will not fit the pictures.

This is how, sometimes, voices make hundreds of pounds in one day, but it is no good, long term, because the clients, even though it is their own fault, will not be eager to make foreign versions again. We have had an example of that very problem recently. The client asked originally for the full service, translations, voices and studio for two productions, one for a film, the other for an audio recording only. The languages were German, Italian and Spanish, the sort of projects we work on all the time in relatively easy languages. The cost was sent to the clients and nothing happened for quite a few weeks, so long in fact, that we thought the project had been shelved altogether. No, the client came back and said: "Ok, we have the translations, we have the voices, could you provide us with the studio and a language specialist to listen in during the recording to make sure the voices read the script and also maybe to help if there are a couple of little problems to iron out." Well, yes, we could do that, we could find native speakers with experience at directing voices in a studio and also experts in linguistics. There was a bit of haggling about the cost of the linguistic advisors but we were given the go-ahead.

The German and the Spanish worked reasonably well, it only took half an hour more than if we had done it all ourselves, but that is not bad going; the clients must have been lucky at gambling and the Russian Roulette was firing blanks! Lucky once, lucky twice, but unlucky the third time around. The Italian was a disaster. The style of the script was wrong and far too long, no way could the recording be made within the hour, not even with the additional thirty minutes of studio time we had reserved for an emergency and that were used for the other two languages. It was a Friday, so the linguistic advisor explained to the client on the phone (by the way the company did not bother to send a representative to the studio; being based outside London it would have cost a lot on travel and travel time), so the advisor explained that she could just about rewrite the script over the weekend if they wanted to and that then the rest of the two programmes could be recorded on the Monday. The cost of the rewrite was passed on to the client and by six o'clock on the Friday evening no decision had been made.

On Monday the client called and said they did not need the translation to be redone, that they did not need the services of the linguistic advisor either and that they would like to finish the recording on the Tuesday. The voice was duly booked for the Tuesday afternoon for an hour; with a little warning from us that it would be good if he did not plan something else for his early evening as the session was starting at five p.m. The client was on the phone listening to the recording, not understanding a word of Italian. The translation was the same and the voice on his own started the slow process of rewriting the script "live" in the studio to make it fit to the pictures. As a result it took another three hours to finish the session. The script fitted, but it was not as good as if it had been written professionally in the first place; one just cannot do that in the heat of the moment and under great pressure. Oh, and by the way at six p.m. the client said: "I am not staying, I have to go home now!" Not that that person was of any use, apart from the moral support and the fact that someone from the company could hear what was going on and that we were doing our best to get them out of the hole they had dug for themselves. Another thing, did you notice how these programmes which had to be finished by Friday evening at the latest were suddenly given an additional four days before completion? I will give you a precise idea of the amount of money the client wasted on this operation because they did not do it properly. The cost of the translation to the client once it had been increased on the way by the agency and the production company would have been about £250 to £300. The cost of recording it in the studio with a professional voice in one hour and again with the mark up from the agency and the production company would have been about £350. In reality it took another three and a half hours, so the total waste for the client was, for these two relatively short programmes, £1225! Do I need to add anything to that!? An investment of a maximum of £300 in the translation would have saved that company £1225! And they were lucky twice; imagine if they had been unlucky!

On this very matter of saving a few pennies I want to print here a quote from a client for whom we translated into eleven languages, but for some reason they decided not to give us the Latin American Spanish. Here is what the charming client from Scandinavia wrote on the eve of the recording, which happened to be a Bank Holiday in England: *"We still haven't got the Lat. Spanish text ready. Have you scheduled recordings of all languages for tomorrow? I was hoping the Lat. Spanish was on Wednesday. If we can't get the text to you we will have to cancel it at our expense.* **I assure you: next time we will let you translate that one too. You wouldn't believe the trouble I've had."**

Well, actually I do believe her. How much could that company have saved on a £200 translation? If the translation does not arrive in time, there will be a studio and artist cancellation charge which might very well be £200! And we don't know if it is going to fit or be in the right style, but I have been through that earlier.

To recap, if you decide to go for our type of translation you cannot really expect to be successful at it if you wish to keep to a nine-to-five schedule and have all your weekends free. The good thing is that you might enjoy some quality time when nobody else is, for example the tennis courts might very well be empty if you decide to go there on a Tuesday morning! It is of course your choice but I wanted you to be aware of what you are letting yourself into if you decide to enter the world of the voice-over.

GENERAL
KNOWLEDGE

There is something else about translating for voice-overs that is also important and this is that you will need to have a very wide general knowledge, as the subject matter in the translations will change very often. As a voice-over specialist, it is very unlikely that you will be able to make a living working in only one field. I don't think you would find enough films about "horses" for example to work exclusively in that field. This is one more reason why I have mentioned earlier that you need to have your scripts checked by someone in the client's company who is a native speaker of your own language.

As a voice-over translator you become a specialist of that style, and of course you might also remain a specialist in certain areas, but you will not be able to cover the full spectrum. Having said that, there will be areas that you will not want to touch because you know very well that you do not understand the subject matter at all and that you do not have the resources to deal with it. Or do you? Well, many of you have friends and colleagues, you belong to numerous networks, you are members of translating associations and professional bodies. So there is a way that works very well. You ask your friend who is a keen horse rider and who contributes translations to a regular monthly publication for help. The problem of course is that this friend is going to give you a translation that is far too long and in the wrong style; this is where your own expertise of writing for voice-overs comes in. You rewrite the script to fit the picture and to fit the spoken style. Oh yes I can see you jumping in your seat and wanting to object. I know what the objections are. I have told you many times that the client is in a hurry to get his translation for the next day. Well, you can try to negotiate on that and get a bit more time, or work through the night to get it done. The second objection is that the cost is going to be higher, well yes so you need to ask for a bit more money or a lot as the case may be, and then share with your friends and colleagues.

I have probably not answered all your questions, but I hope you can now see the big picture and that you will be able to embark on a successful career as a translator of the spoken word. ___Any comments or questions would be welcomed.___

To end this part about translating I would like to quote from George Orwell who published an essay called *Politics and the English Language*. He was not thinking about translating or writing voice-overs but he made a point relevant to our type of translation. He was complaining about the evolution of the English language. He took a very well-known and very clearly written example from Ecclesiastes in the 1611 King James version of the Bible – itself a translation from the Hebrew, of course and then "translated" it into modern English:

> "*I returned, and saw under the sun, that the race is not to the swift, nor the battle to the strong, neither yet bread to the wise, nor yet riches to men understanding, nor yet favour to men of skill; but time and chance happeneth to them all.*"

And here is his version in modern English:

> "*Objective consideration of contemporary phenomena compels the conclusion that success or failure in competitive activities exhibits no tendency to be commensurate with innate capacity, but that a considerable element of the unpredictable must invariably be taken into account.*"

He goes on to analyse the two sentences and explains that the first one contains forty-nine words but only sixty syllables and that all the words are those used in everyday life. The second contains thirty-eight words but has ninety syllables. In other words modern English uses long difficult words which have a tendency to render the message more difficult to decipher. A translator of the spoken word should in my opinion try to emulate the first type of writing. OK, I don't mean that you have to use the equivalent of archaic forms of English like "happeneth" in your translations, but simplification and clarity are paramount if you wish the message to be understood. However, this is not always in our hands as the client might not wish that to be the case, but we can always hope!

FORMATTING
THE SCRIPT

In order to make it easier for the voice to read, an appropriate presentation of the script is always helpful. Using half the page vertically for example means that the eye does not have to travel so far from the end of the line to the beginning of the next one; this makes it easier to read in a more fluent way. It is not unusual for voices to be surprised by what is coming next on the following line. When that happens, there might be a hesitation or the inflection might be wrong and a retake of the sentence or the paragraph will be needed. Very often the script is indeed presented in two or three columns, one with the time codes, one with the original script and one with the translation, as mentioned before.

This presentation provides numerous advantages. It gives you an instant picture of the length situation. Also if there is a problem with the translation while recording, the voice can refer back instantaneously to the original script, and make the necessary changes. It is also a good idea to use a point size large enough to help people who might not have 20/20 vision. I wonder if my age is telling me something here! Another important point is not to cut a sentence at the end of a page. It is well worth using a few more pages for the script. If you make sure that the end of a page is also the end of a paragraph or at the very least the end of a sentence, it will be easier for the voice to turn to the next page without making any paper rustle at the wrong time.

These seem to be small points but at the end of the day they can make quite a difference in the way the session goes. When I say use more pages, I am not trying to kill even more trees than is necessary. I do my best to save paper by using both sides of the sheet, but you should never use both side for a script that you are going to read in a studio as it would be impossible to turn the page without making any noise. I use the second side for any internal printing that is required; in fact I very often bring back the scripts from the studios and use the other side in the office. It is sometimes a little bit boring as paper which has already been used tends to jam a bit more often in printers than brand new paper, but thinking of the trees makes up for it!

Or is that true? I was in very large company not too long ago and there was this fantastic state-of-the-art printer and having to wait for my meeting I got chatting to someone making copies. After a little while the person explained that the machine was superb and that people could send scripts to be printed while they were in their offices and come back a few minutes later to collect the pages, but she added: "The problem is that the paper jams and there are queues of scripts to be printed in the system, and we are in a mess. It happens almost every day!" And of course as a large company, they were not going to use the other side of the sheets of paper; they were using paper coming straight out of the box. I felt reassured then and decided I would carry on…saving trees.

SUBTITLING

The technical parameters

Once involved in translating corporate material, you will no doubt be asked by your clients, at one stage or another, if you could also help with subtitles. I am going to talk about subtitles of corporate videos or training material, not of feature films where the parameters are not quite the same. This is a translation style that is totally different from the spoken style I have been speaking about earlier.

However, some of the comments I made before still apply here. For example, many of the factors involved in translating for voice-overs will also affect the translation of subtitles, like the urgency, the freedom to adapt the script, the aptitude to translate the thoughts rather than the words. The time constraints will also be of the utmost importance in this type of translation and time codes will be used.

There are three different scenarios you might be confronted with when asked to translate subtitles. You might be asked to go to the client's office and work using their equipment. They will probably train you, or at least show you how to operate their computer, so that you can very quickly concentrate on the actual translation work. In this case all the technical parameters should be taken care of and that aspect of your work should be relatively easy.

The second scenario is when you are asked to work with your own word-processing package from your study. You will be sent existing subtitles to translate. It is what we call a spotting list.

And the third possibility is that you will be sent a full transcript of the production and you will have to make the spotting list yourself as well as the translation.

A spotting list contains a large number of characters for the encoding of the file in the subtitling software. There are a maximum of two lines of subtitles and the number of characters will not exceed forty including punctuation and spaces. Here is an example of what a spotting list looks like.

0011 : 10:00:51:08,10:00:52:28,10
80 80 80
C1N03 Here are our main stories.
0012 : 10:00:55:00,10:00:56:20,10
80 80 80
C1N03 The first flight over Paris…
0013 : 10:00:56:24,10:01:00:26,10
80 80 80
C1N03…of the world's largest passenger
C1N03 aircraft, the Airbus A380.

Table 11

You will notice that there is a large number of characters on the first two lines which are in fact codes telling the subtitling software what to do. The first four characters indicate the number of the subtitle. In the example above 0011 indicates that this subtitle is number eleven (in this production, we had over 500 subtitles). The rest of the line is made up of time codes, the ones I have told you about before and which will tell the equipment exactly when the subtitles should appear and disappear. Look at the rest of the line (10:00:56:24,10:01:00:26), it is imperative that these are strictly adhered to, or the file will fail technically. There are two sets of 8 figures; they indicate the beginning and the end of the subtitle. (You should therefore never tamper with these figures.) The 10 stands for the hour, it does not mean that the film is 10 hours long. The production probably started at 10 hours. 00 show the minutes, we are at the beginning of the film in this example. 56 are the seconds and the last two the frames. On this one you can see that the subtitle is going to stay on screen for just under 4 seconds. When I said you have 40 characters for each line you must not include the C1 N03 and the spaces in between and after. You start counting the characters, if you take subtitle 0011 for example, with the letter H. If you are using Word, you will not have to count the characters manually. You will put the cursor after the full stop and you will see at the bottom of the page the number of the Col (column) you are at, you subtract 7 (the number of code and spaces), and you have the length of your subtitle. I did not think I would have to spell out this part of the job in so many details, but I recently received a script back from a client complaining that we had done a bad job, that many of the subtitles were far too long. It was a long script and he must have taken a lot of time to change the subtitles, creating a third line in some cases. We very quickly worked out that he had not subtracted the seven encoding characters. So, nothing must be assumed. In my defence I would say that we had been told that this reviewer had done that sort of work before, but here we are. I had to spend a number of hours to rectify his version of the subtitles. The only thing we wanted from him was to make sure that we had used the right technical terms and the in-house jargon and that he would make changes accordingly, not to re-edit our subtitles which fitted very well, thank you very much!

The third possibility is that you will receive a full script to make into subtitles. That is when you will have to make your own spotting list. You will need to decide where each subtitle starts and finishes. You have, of course, not forgotten to ask the client how long each subtitle should remain in vision, how many lines you are allowed to use and how many characters you can have for each line. You will also have asked for a VHS with time codes in vision so that you can write down when the subtitles can start and finish. As mentioned before about voice-overs, you will not need to concern yourself with frame numbers, the seconds will be enough. The specialist entering the subtitles in the system will fine tune to the frame when necessary. You therefore need to look at the film carefully when you do this exercise. For example, try to avoid having a subtitle remaining on screen over a picture cut. A picture cut happens when one scene changes to another. Also try and ensure that grammatical clauses remain together, without single words "hanging over" between subtitles. You must also pay particular attention to existing captions, such as titles, names of people and bullet points, appearing on screen.

I remember an instance when we subtitled a video into Arabic. Arabic is already naturally much longer than English so it is a real challenge to make Arabic subtitles. In that case we also had a number of personalities being interviewed; they not only had long names, but also long titles, like "His Excellency the Emir of so and so" and of course when they appear they start speaking straight away. The captions pops up at the same time and you have to display the subtitles and the viewers need to have time to read the lot. It does not look very good if everything is packed up on the television screen at the same time. The editing and spotting become of the utmost importance in this case. Something has to be cut. There is no way the names and titles can be shortened, so the speech has to be condensed in such a way that the meaning is not lost even if some of the words are. I must admit that we had to fine tune considerably in the edit suite to achieve something acceptable in that instance; in the end it all worked pretty well. We gained half a second here, half a second there, we had the captions in one corner and the subtitles coming in at the bottom a fraction of a second before the caption disappeared, that sort of thing. However, this was unusual, in that the edit suite had a subtitling operative readily available to fine-tune the changes. It was an extreme case, but this is the reality of translating subtitles.

So once the spotting has been agreed, you can start on the translation itself. If you follow the rules I have established you should be able to make reasonably good subtitles. However, you might very well be confronted with a challenge. You might not even be given the film and be asked to cut the full script into subtitles. This will undoubtedly result in a very poor production. The viewers will probably spend all their time reading the subtitles and not seeing the film, or even worse will not even have the time to read them all.

This is why a spotting list should be created before you start translating. That will have to be done by your client or by yourself. The spotting list is the creation of English subtitles, or subtitles in whatever language the original film has been produced. The film producer, director or writer will have to decide not only that the subtitles must respect the two-line and forty-character rules but also include the minimum time each subtitle must stay on screen to give the audience time to read them. This time will vary depending on the target audience. It is likely that less time will be allocated for each subtitle for an audience of people in the professions say, than to an audience of mechanics. It could be anything between roughly four and six or seven seconds. For a one-liner it is going to be shorter than for a two-liner and the length of the subtitles will also determine the length of time it will stay on the screen. Two short lines will be read much faster than two lines of forty characters each. It is also easier to read a "short fat" subtitle, whereby two even lines are achieved, rather than a "top heavy" subtitle, which may only have one word on the bottom. I must reiterate that it is always better if the client does that sort of work, or if a specialist subtitler is involved at this stage. The added advantage is that the client or the film director can retain editorial control of what is important and what is less important as some words will have to go. It also makes economic sense for the client, especially if more than one language version has to be translated. Otherwise, each translator will have to make a spotting list and charge accordingly. It is a time-consuming exercise and it must be charged on top of your translating rate. If you find yourself in this situation I would strongly recommend that you ask your client to approve your spotting list before you start working on the translation.

In an ideal world you would always want to have a look at the film before starting on the translation for all the reasons I mentioned before. You know you already have many technical constraints and it would be nice also to have a feel for the film before starting your work. It might also be extremely useful for something as mundane as understanding the basic message. I have had endless cases where a very difficult sentence, or even words, to translate became obvious with the picture in front of me; the body language is sometimes vital in order to understand what a person is saying. In real life it does not always happen. In such a case I try to obtain a full transcript of the film in order to have as much background information as possible. I have to admit that with subjects you know well and for styles of films you have worked on often, it is possible to translate subtitles on their own, without watching the film and without the full script, but it is not ideal and I would certainly not advise you to do that if you have not had a lot of experience in translating subtitles or for that matter voice-over scripts. In some languages, if not all languages, it is very important to know if the person speaking is male or female. If you have not seen the film and you don't have the full script, and work only from the spotting list, you might no be able to work out if the person speaking on screen is a man or a woman. If you cannot watch the film you need to ask for a breakdown of who's who in the film. The production might lose its credibility if the wrong gender has been used in the subtitles.

Now we have to come to the nitty-gritty of it. The way I handle the translation is to look at a full sequence, by which I mean a full sentence in the original subtitles. I need to work out what the message of the sentence is, what the main idea is, and then start translating the idea rather than the words. Say you have three subtitles to translate this idea. You start your translation but you discover that instead of six lines, you have seven, but it looks like the first line of the first subtitle is very short because of a long word that wraps to the next line. That's when the fun starts. You need to juggle with your own language, with the grammar, with the word order to make sure you make as much use as possible of the forty characters. You might have to look for synonyms, you might find a word which is shorter by one letter or two and that might make all the difference. Letter width is also important: w is wider than l, so if you have many "l"s or "i"s in a subtitle you might get away with one or two more characters. All these little things will help you. You might also change the logic of the sentence by turning it around, in a way not dissimilar to the example given earlier in Korean with the names of the film stars and the film directors. The most difficult subtitles to translate are the ones where an entire sentence is reduced to one subtitle; you must really put your thinking cap on for these ones. It is a little bit like when you have to translate a short statement for a voice-over which is only two or three seconds long; with a twenty-second speech, there is always a little bit of leeway to make everything fit.

Sometimes the translation is rendered even more difficult when clients insist on using a specific word which is longer than another one you would prefer, and, to add to the difficulty, that word might recur quite often in the script. You have to take into account this added complication in your translation. There is no way you can add characters to the number given by the client. And modifying the size of the font is not going to help either. The reason why the number of characters is limited to forty is that otherwise they might disappear off screen. We make sure this way it is "television safe". I know I have said that you cannot change the font and the size of the font, but the subtitler will have chosen the font and its size and this is why it is quite useful to ask every time how many lines and how many characters you are allowed to use; it can indeed vary a little bit, but not much. The professional subtitler will decide on the size of the font which will in turn dictate the number of characters. The danger is of course that if the font size is too small, viewers will not be able to read the subtitles. Whatever the number of lines and the number of characters, the client will have to accept that not everything can be translated and that shortcuts will be required. Sometimes, abbreviations can be used as long as they are well known to the target audience.

Every now and again, you might be asked to produce subtitles which will run across the bottom of the screen. These are completely different; they tend to be a verbatim translation of what is said on screen. It is very difficult for the viewer to read them and it is very distracting. The viewer will find it very difficult to read them all and watch the pictures as well. They tend to be used when the pictures are pretty static, like company results, forms and the like. You see them appear on TV stations specialising in finance for example. They are not ideal, far from it, for a corporate video and are very seldom used.

I also need to emphasise that it is vital that your spelling should be spotless; there is nothing much worse than typos in subtitles.

Spelling

I would like to add a little note about spelling here. It is not a problem for most professional translators, but some of the voices who do their own translations have a tendency not to worry too much about the way they spell. They tell me, "Oh yes I know, I don't have a spell-checker and I am the one who is going to read the script, so it's OK!" This is also something I have encountered with some of the interpreters who do not have to write on paper very often. In theory this is of course not a big problem as long as it does not affect their pronunciation and that the words and the sentences **sound** right. However, it is not very good practice because the scripts will very often be checked by the end clients (as I said before they should **always** be checked by the end clients) who might get most upset by the number of corrections they need to make. Remember that these people are more used to reading manuals, magazines and the like, and they will not take lightly to what they will consider, quite rightly, as a sloppy translation. It will become much more difficult for translators to defend or justify their work if clients start questioning the quality of the translation. The typos will be the first thing they see and they will then look for what else could be wrong. They will not "trust" the integrity of the translators and think that if they have left typos, they might not have been very thorough with the rest of the script either. Spelling is like a first impression. If it is bad, it is going to be very difficult to rectify it in the future.

Dubbing or subtitling?

This question is discussed all the time by translators, voice-overs and of course filmgoers. The point of view will vary greatly depending on your culture. In Scandinavia, The Netherlands and Belgium for example, subtitles are used extensively on many productions, including feature films, television series and corporate productions. I remember travelling around Europe with my rucksack on my back in the late '60s and being astonished when I went into a cinema in Belgium to watch an English language film. The subtitles there were not only in French but also in Flemish on the same screen! On that same trip I was given a lift by a Dutchman who could speak six languages. To me this was inconceivable; I could hardly cope with English at the time. And then I met a boy of seven or eight in Luxembourg, I think he was the son of the Youth Hostel father[1], and he could already speak four languages! I must say that these early experiences stimulated me greatly to learn languages; in fact I wanted to learn all of the Common Market languages. Mind you at the time there were only six member countries and the languages were Dutch, French, German and Italian with varieties of Dutch and German being spoken in Belgium and Luxembourg. I have a long way to go now that we have twenty-seven countries in the Union!

But back to subtitles! In the countries where they are part of the culture and where people watch films in their original version as a matter of course, people tend to have good accents. This is because they pick up the languages by listening to them. The other advantage is that they can appreciate more fully the feelings expressed by the actors. In countries like France and Italy to take another example, original versions are appreciated by a few who like to watch quality productions in the original. The majority of people, however, in theses countries will never see a film in the original language, they will watch dubbed productions.

As it happens, the French and the Italians (and I am not especially picking on them, there are others in exactly the same situation) have quite strong accents when they speak foreign languages. But, some of them will redeem themselves by having a good grasp of the grammar of the foreign language. As a Frenchman I am always in awe of the Swedes when they speak English. Their accent is really superb and I am always impressed when I hear them. However, one day, I had to transcribe a managing director's speech. It sounded really great, but when I started to put the words on paper, I realised that his grammar was not that good, and certainly not to the level I expected from someone speaking with such a beautiful accent and occupying such a high position in a major company. On the other hand a French school friend of mine had written a remarkable essay on his subject (he is an authority on salmon) and had to read it at an international conference in the North of England. On his way he stopped in London and asked me to check it for him. I was amazed at the quality of his written English, and yet he was hardly able to order a cup of coffee in a restaurant!

The French, and I would suspect all the other peoples who prefer dubbed films, tend to think that if they want to read something they take a book, a magazine or a brochure. When they go to the "pictures", well, they want to see pictures! However, in the corporate sector other factors come into play. Even though French, Germans, Italians and Spaniards do not like to read subtitles, some companies will provide them with subtitled training material rather than dubbed videos. The reason is very simple; it is cheaper to make subtitles than to do a proper dubbing. However, it is in my view the wrong decision to make. It is always hard to train people; with the best will in the world managers find it hard to make time for training and if on top of it they have to contend with a product that goes against the grain, it is even more difficult. The bottom line is that you might be making savings in the short term by using subtitles, but are in fact wasting money in the long term because your message will not be relayed to the intended audience and the training will not be as effective as it could have been.

The debate could go on and on and in fact does go on and go on amongst film aficionados.

---

1   In the Youth Hostel organisation the manager was known as the Father, when I was young and used these hostels all around Europe!

THE WORK OF
THE "VOICE"

I started voicing in the '70s when we were still using film as a support. It was easier than when narrations or songs were recorded on wax because then there was only one take from beginning to end and there was no way that you could edit the recordings. Even in the '70s good preparation was essential for a good session. If the groundwork had not been done properly the session would overrun dramatically. The cost escalated to the great displeasure of the client. It was impossible for the client to provide the translator with a copy of the film as nobody had the equipment at home to watch it anyway. Reels of film were bulky and copies cost a lot of money. Therefore clients had to provide a very detailed script and they normally did have one because it was needed to work on their own original version. It was called the post production script. In order to edit the film and the sound together they required a marked-up script, with all the "timings" and the scene descriptions – the expression "time codes" was not used then. The translators therefore worked from such scripts. If they had experience in radio or were actors they would time themselves while writing the foreign version and the session in the studio would be successful.

However, just as now, many of the translators did not have these skills and the foreign scripts were too long. I must say that it was very often the case and I have had on countless occasions to rewrite, edit and shorten the script while the client was getting hot under the collar. Admittedly they were good times for the voices with the required talents for translating or writing as we were paid by the time spent in the studio. The added bonus was that clients asked us to write their next script to avoid having problems in the studio. I picked up hundreds of new clients this way and many of my colleagues did the same.

This situation prevailed until the '80s, as things eased up a bit for the translators with the advent of video. It then became a bit easier to edit the pictures and therefore sometimes (but not always, far from it) clients would be happy enough to reedit the pictures for a better result, whereas they would never have "recut" the film. Once the battle of Betacam versus VHS was definitely won by the latter, all translators specialising in voice work had acquired a video player and were able, in theory, to watch the films they were asked to translate. I say *in theory* because very often the films were not sent for all sorts of reasons. Clients still had to get used to sending their films to translators as it wasn't part of their modus operandi. There were, and still are, the pressures of time and money, as to send the VHS delayed matters by another day or two if it had to go by post, and delivery by courier is still expensive, or perhaps the film was not quite ready. Even though it was technically possible to watch the video to do the translation, it did not always happen.

When recording for a film we were given cue lights, green or red, depending on the studio, which was sometimes confusing for some of us, as many people had the tendency to stop at the "red" and start at the "green". But we were not on the highway and whatever the colour, it only meant we had to start reading the next paragraph. (The reason the lights are switched on is to indicate to other people in the building that a recording is on and that they should not barge in or make too much noise outside the studio doors.) If the script was written correctly to time, it was a doddle, a "piece of cake". It was very easy work: one only had to concentrate on the light and the script and maybe keep an eye on the film to see if fine-tuning could be achieved by hitting some internal cues, like "explosions", "door closing", "engine starting" as I said earlier, and so on, if they had not been written in the script. However, with the possibility of playing the original track in the "cans" (jargon for "headphones"), it became possible for the voice to listen to the original track and read the foreign script alongside it. Directors became lazy and started to rely on this method more and more. This way they did not have to press the button for cue lights. Anyway there was a little problem about the cue light. Light travels fast, but the finger of the director, the eyesight of the voice and the time for the voice to start speaking created a delay. In theory that should not have been a problem in itself as the editor could have moved the recording back by the length of the delay and everything would have fallen into place. However, the delay was not always of the same length, not only did it vary from one voice to another, but also for the same voice sometimes. Some people were sharp off the mark a few times but then their reaction time lengthened. Or they might have been slow at the beginning and as the recording progressed would start to get faster. The same type of thing happened to directors; they might be distracted by all sorts of things in the studio environment, something which had not been spotted on the film before, or a phone call coming in, or the studio engineer telling them something. So the possibility of letting the voice be in charge of the timing by listening to the guide track had great appeal to them. We therefore had to develop this new skill of listening to one language and speaking in our native tongue at the same time. The challenge there is to make sure you can split your brain into two parts, the listening one and the speaking one. One has to be extremely careful to retain the rhythm of the native language and not become unduly influenced in the delivery by the original version. That is when you realise you have to use **both** ears so to speak, one to listen to the original track and the other to listen to your own voice. In some studios the two tracks will be split so that you get the original track in one "can" and your own voice in the other, however, very often we have to listen to both voices.

The way not to get confused was, and very often still is, to have the two voices sent to your ears at different levels. Some people like to hear their own voice very loud and the original track quite low or vice versa. Some time is spent at the beginning of each session to set the levels so that the artist feels comfortable.

First is the level at which the sound engineer wants to record your voice on the "computer". (No more recording on 16mm film or quarter inch "reel-to-reel" or 16 track or 32 track machines. You can still see some of these machines in studios, but they are very rarely used and are kept, I think, purely out of nostalgia for the "good old days"!)

Reel-to-reel machine OTARI-MTR-10. The spool on the right is 10.5 inch, for which you use the NAB adaptor; this is the black round object in the middle of the spool. The one on the left is 7 inch, hence the unused NAB adaptor on top of the monitoring bridge.

Secondly, some time is also spent setting the levels in the "cans". Everyone is different and a good balance for each voice must be achieved. This is the balance between the original track that is going to be used as a guide and the return of your own voice for you to check that you are happy with what you are recording. Do not be put off by the time this can take. It is well worth spending five minutes or more to set these right as the entire quality of the recording will depend on them. You might even find out, after a couple of minutes' recording that, after all, you need a bit more of the original track or a bit less, or that in fact you cannot quite hear your own voice the way you would like to. Do not hesitate to stop and ask the engineer to reset the levels. The only limitation on the level in the "cans" is caused by something called "bleeding", that is when the level in the earphones (another word for headphones) is so high that it comes out of the headphones and is picked up by the microphone and is being recorded as well as your original voice. This can be rectified by using better headphones in some instances, and studios will very quickly find out if they need to equip themselves better if this "bleeding" is happening with everybody. However, in most cases it happens when a voice is either hard of hearing or needs to have the sound very high in the cans to work well. For people with hearing difficulties, the solution is of course to see a specialist and have some sort of hearing aid fitted so that you do not have to ask for the levels to be too high. If it is only because you like to hear the sound of the original track or of your own voice very high, I am afraid you will need to retrain yourself to work with slightly lower levels. It can be done and I have seen quite a few artists dealing successfully with this problem.

The voice works as an actor when reading the script. He or she concentrates on the delivery, making sure that the words carry the right meaning. The interpretation is also very important; one must not forget that the voice must have authority and must be convincing. It becomes the voice of the company and as well as authoritative and convincing it must be warm and friendly. One of the tricks that artists sometimes find difficult to negotiate is to give the impression that they are knowledgeable: the reading must be such that the listeners believe that the person reading knows all about the subject, but I must tell you, between you and me, this is rarely the case. One day I might be asked to read about safety on North Sea Oil platforms and the next about a new type of heart operation. *Yes*, a vast general knowledge *is* useful, but really, in most cases, we only know a little bit about many different subjects, we only scratch the surface! So the artist must have the knack of understanding quickly, I would say spontaneously, which words need to be emphasized, which words are the important ones in a sentence.

You will tell me: "But certainly you receive the script before and you can find out what it is all about and practice, you might be able to mark your script and you should not have any problems!" Dream on! More often than not we are required to **sight**-read. In 2004 I spent over five hundred hours in a studio for a single client recording on average 4,000 to 4,500 words an hour. There was no way I would have read the scripts before going into the studio. To read them once was arduous enough! In any case the scripts were only delivered to the studio at the last minute. This speed of **sight**-reading is only possible when recording audio only and with no time constraint; it would have taken three to four times as long if the words had to fit to pictures and that estimate is only valid if the scripts had been written to fit the pictures! Giving the impression of understanding the script is essential. I remember one instance of someone from a multinational coming to me and asking me in which department of his company I was working? To me that was worth an Oscar! Another company director told me one day: "From now on you are going to be the voice of our company!"

Sight-reading is the aim to be achieved by voices. Having said that, there are some good readers who are not quite able to walk into the studio, sit down in front of the script and read it because of the nature of their language. In Arabic for example, most readers have to mark their script, as the verbs are not typed the way they are going to be read. Only very experienced readers who do it every day and have done it for a long time can **sight**-read. Some of the Italians find it important to mark the stresses on their scripts as well, and the time used to do that in the studio, if the script has not be sent to them before, is recouped by the speed of the recording afterwards. Of course, if the scripts are very long, marking scripts up will make the sessions longer than with voices who don't need to do that. So even in Italian and Arabic, the aim is to become a good **sight**-reader.

There are languages where "reading" and "writing" are not very natural. For example, Somali[1] has only become a written language in the past few decades; it is traditionally an oral language. The Somali voice I worked with impressed me as being a perfect voice-over artist. Not a **sight**-reader, as he did not read the script. We had taken great care to have the script translated and when he came to the studio, he said, "No I don't want to read the Somali, I will read from the English." I thought the director was going to have a heart attack and fortunately I was sitting down when he said that! We thought he was going to deliver his script the way some simultaneous interpreters do it sometimes in a very monotonous voice. But no, he was looking at the English and his brain was processing the script and it came out in lively Somali, or at least that is the way it sounded in the studio. To our amazement it also fitted the format pretty well and not much more editing was required than for the average voice-over. And to cap it all the end user was very happy! I have to say that this gentleman has a daily experience of reading from English into Somali and has done so for many years; even in Somalia, not many people would be as proficient at this sort of exercise as he is! So every language has its idiosyncrasies, but sight-reading is still the norm and a skill you will need to acquire.

So you are reading your script, but even the best will at one stage or another fluff a word and have to restart the recording. Something might happen to the computer; they do crash, it is quite usual. (However, today's computers are so well designed that most of the time nothing is lost, so it is only a question of taking a breather, giving you a chance to relax for a few minutes while the computer reboots. In some studios where the engineers do not trust computers one hundred per cent, they make a DAT [Digital Audio Tape] back-up of the entire session. This can be very useful in more ways than one. Something dramatic might happen to the computer and the entire session could be lost; it is rare but it could happen. Some clients who like to have many takes of the same sentence also like to take the DAT with them so that they can, if they wish, replace one of the sentences at a later stage.) The engineer might have done something wrong and we need to restart.

There are a couple of different ways this will work. The most common one is to stop, agree on where you go back to. It could be the beginning of the previous sentence or the top of the paragraph or it could even be in the middle of a sentence. You will then have to do a drop-in. You will hear what you have recorded before and start speaking naturally at the right moment, not too soon, not too late. If you start too soon, your voice might be clipped, if you start too late, it is not a problem nowadays as the engineer will be able to move you back to the right place "on the fly", if he is good and if using the right software, or else it will be done at the editing stage.

On some more rudimentary equipment used in a large number of small studios, mainly for audio recordings only, once the starting point has been established you will be told when to start or a light will be given to you to start your recording at that place. There are also cases when the engineer is asked by the client to record the entire session and the editing will be done once you have gone. In that case, you must always go back to a very distinctive place. The beginning of a sentence or a paragraph; you should not restart in the middle of a sentence.

Or you might be asked to identify your retakes in English so that the editor will know where to edit. In some instances when you are doing very long sessions and there are some very long sentences, it is possible to drop in the middle of sentences, especially if you have been struggling with one word and you have just managed to read it correctly and a couple of words later you stumble on an easy one. That will only be done if the breathing is right, if the studio engineer is confident and if he or she and you can drop in properly. In such an instance it is advisable to do so, and the studio manager will probably ask you to double-check that the drop-in is good before proceeding to the next paragraph.

In the old days, it was pretty difficult to drop in when recording on film. You had to leave just enough space so that it sounded natural. Every drop-in was checked at the end of the paragraph. We always used to listen back to the entire production to make sure everything was "ticketyboo" as well. (I remember a little anecdote of these long gone times. A studio manager told me that he had once worked with a very crafty guy who never wanted to retake anything because he could not admit he had made a mistake. While listening back to the film he would cough when a fluff was coming up, trying to hide his error to the people in the studio. It was of course considered to be very unprofessional and this guy did not stay in this business for very long!) However, if there were corrections to be made, it could take quite a bit of time. We had to identify exactly what had to be redone. The studio engineer had to know exactly where to drop in and where to drop out. The danger was that you could start too early or overrun and erase the beginning of the next sentence or paragraph. It was all done "live" so to speak. The tendency was to read the retake a little bit faster than the original, just to make sure it would fit in the allocated space.

An improvement came when the engineer was able to set entry and exit points so that at least you could not overwrite what had been recorded previously. Compared to the way we work now it all seems very amateurish, but we were at the forefront of technology even then!

As well as being an actor, a script writer, a language specialist and an editor, the voice will very often be asked to be his own director. In most recording sessions, the voice is the only native speaker of the language; on rare occasions there might be someone who might understand the language a little bit. As the only native speaker, you therefore need to make sure that you are recording the right words. The first thing is to make sure you are reading what is in the script, with the proviso that the script makes sense and that you are not changing some words on purpose. Then you must be convinced that you are reading the words with the right feeling, the right emphasis and that the message is carried the way it should be. Of course all that is being done at the same time. You are listening to the original track to know where you are, you are reading your script and you are listening to your own voice. A tall order! However, if you have one hour in the studio to record up to about fifteen minutes of finished film, you should have the time to listen back to yourself and make any necessary corrections. This is a very important part of the job as everyone can make a mistake when so many things are happening at the same time.

I have recently had an example of that, when a young lady made a wrong *liaison* in French and did not realise it; it was broadcast with that *liaison*, until the mistake was discovered by chance and corrected a couple of weeks later, but it had already gone on air.

So I would always recommend you take the time to listen back to your own recording, even if the engineer speaks your own language. The engineer is not listening to the script as such, he is listening for many other technical things, little noises you might make, interference that might come into the systems, studio cricks or idiosyncrasies. I even remember recording in BBC Broadcasting House in one of the basement studios where we could hear the noise of the Tube under the ground! The engineer will also make sure you do not pop and that your levels are constant, so his or her brain will hardly have time to analyse the script for its meaning; that is your responsibility. This makes it tight: there is no time to lose in a one-hour session and therefore you cannot arrive late at the session, as every minute counts. If the client arrives late, if there is a breakdown in the studio, then it is not your responsibility any longer and if it takes a few more minutes than the expected hour, you will base your decision of charging more on the circumstances, your relationship with the clients and their attitude. (In the '70s we used to charge a full hour after the end of the first hour in the studio, but it is not done anymore. After the first hour, only half an hour is charged. I am reluctant to go any further and split it in quarters of an hour, but the pressure is on.)

In the '70s we allowed a full hour for a ten-minute film. The reasons being that technology was slower, the entire process was slower. The stopping and drop-in were slower, the playback of the full film was slower, it took quite some time to wind back to the beginning of the recording; if one made a mistake the repair was a tricky business. The voice therefore assumes a number of responsibilities when he goes into a "recording suite". (This is quite a grand expression for a studio, but I think it is justified as there are very different types of studios around. One would probably go into a "recording suite" to voice a commercial, but use a studio to record a training programme or a language course.) You will therefore understand why the fee voices receive is quite high per hour compared to the work done for a translator to translate one thousand words. As such, the fee is of course quite an incentive for translators to want to become voices. They are also a great incentive for actors who might have to work a full week in a theatre to earn the same amount they would make in a couple of hours in a studio.

How to become a voice: establishing what is required

There are quite a number of steps you have to undertake to become a voice. You will need to check a few pre-requisites. I am afraid the first one is to find out if your natural accent in your language is broadly acceptable all over the target country. South American is a good example of where problems can arise. There are about twenty countries in the world where Spanish is the lingua franca; seventeen of them, I think, in the Americas. It would be nice for voices to have companies making seventeen different versions for this region of the globe, but they will never do that, primarily for reasons of cost. Therefore, unless the production is only aimed at one of the Latin American countries, a Cuban accent, say, is very unlikely to be acceptable. It is more likely that someone from Columbia will be asked to do the recording. For some reason, Columbian is considered to be the equivalent to the Queen's English in Latin America. In Europe we encounter the same sort of thing. Someone with a strong accent from Marseilles or Munich will probably not be asked to do a standard voice-over. There are only very few cases when accented languages will be required. In most cases you will be asked by the client if you speak the equivalent of BBC English or the Queen's English also known as RP, Received Pronunciation. So this is the first hurdle to negotiate. If you have assessed that your accent is reasonably neutral and that you can, if required, put on a regional accent, then that is a good start. But if you have a strong accent in your native tongue, all is not lost. You might, through hard work, lose it. I will say more about that when telling you about the training of your voice.

Having said all that, it is now possible to hear accented broadcasters for a number of programmes on many radio and television stations. This is certainly the trend in Europe. However, the accent tends not to be strong and the voice still sounds reasonably well educated. But to come back to my point; most of the work done in the United Kingdom in foreign languages is being done by people who do not have a regional accent. The reason is quite simple. If you make a programme about a British invention and wish to make a German version, you will want to keep your options open and have a voice that will be acceptable wherever German is spoken, including Austria and Switzerland. The situation would be different if you were making a programme about Swiss cheese, then *yes,* a Swiss accent would be acceptable in German, even in the North of Germany, for example, as this would be part of the product, so to speak.

Also, you must be sure you know exactly which kind of style and intonations are expected. For instance, in Italy, like in most countries, the voices you hear on radio or television have a very specific kind of delivery. That's what the listeners expect, what the clients want and you must be able to do it, unless you're a celebrity or you're specifically asked to be "unconventional". Therefore it is quite useful, when possible, actually to listen to original material broadcast in the countries where your voice is going to be heard. Particularly when it comes to commercials, originality is only appreciated within certain limits.

The other thing you need to find out is quite simply if you can actually **read**. I mean read aloud. I am not joking; there are even professional actors who cannot read. They can learn a part, a couple of pages even, in an hour and give a very impressive performance, but they cannot **sight**-read. I remember very well the case of a friend of mine who is a good actor. He had come to my office one day to rehearse for a corporate video we were going to do. He speaks good French and my English is reasonable so the two of us could record to camera the French and the English versions for a presentation at an international exhibition in Paris. We were having a little break over a cup of coffee when I realised I did not have his demo cassette. I told him about it and he said, "Well *no,* you wouldn't, I can't read!" I just could not believe it, so I asked him to show me and indeed he could not **sight**-read, but he said: "Oh, but I could learn the page in less than thirty minutes!" It turned out that he was put to the test a couple of weeks later when we went for the shoot of the video we had been rehearsing and it was discovered that the director had forgotten one page of script. He did not have any trouble at all learning it over lunch! And it was a pretty technical script at that. So you need to check that you can actually read, without having to prepare for hours for that specific read. It would not work, not when you have hundreds of pages of script to read!

Musicians can sight-read their musical scores: I am always amazed when I see a friend sit at a piano, pick up some music and start to play. Indeed there might be a couple of wrong notes over the few pages being played, just like when one sight-reads a script, one makes a couple of fluffs. So training to sight-read a script requires a lot of preparation, just as in music, if you want to become a professional "player".

How to find out if you can read

The cheap way to check that you can read is to sit in front of a mic connected to a tape recorder or, more likely today, your computer, and then listen to your own voice. You will have to decide if your **voice is clear**, your **elocution is good** and if **you sound convincing**. Beware! If you have never heard your own voice or if you have only heard it a few times, you are going to have a shock, you are going to be very surprised and you are very likely not going to like what you hear. For the first time in your life you are going to hear yourself the way the rest of the world hears you. Do not worry about that, it happens to everybody! So do not judge the sound of your voice by thinking it is too high-pitched or too low or whatever. In any case all types of voices are required for different jobs. Concentrate on the elocution, on the clarity and on being convincing.

If you are not sure, then you could attend a workshop to find out more. Some of them are organised by the different translators' associations from time to time and of course by institutions working with actors. The Actors Centre in London does some training in this respect. Their sight-reading classes and one-to-one voice classes are good, but the problem for foreign translators or actors in London is that they are in English. They could be interesting as a way to discover how to use your voice and how to **sight**-read, but if your English isn't very good and you're not confident acting in English, don't waste your money. Also, don't enrol in expensive "voice-over seminars" that promise to teach you everything and provide you with a demo in one session. They are really overpriced, the demos they produce might look and sound glamorous but they are all the same, and there's no way you can learn to be a voice in one day. You can also try to meet a professional to assess your potential. Go for a recording session and obtain some positive feedback on your performance and on what you will need to do.

Training your voice

The main requirement is the will to invest time and hard work. The first thing to do is of course to read aloud. You must not read fast, you need to read very clearly all the time; this exercise must be done daily for a minimum of ten minutes. Of course the more often you do it, the faster you will achieve proficiency. Ten minutes at a time is good, it is about the length of a news bulletin, so you could do a ten-minute read every hour on the hour, or just a few times a day.

Not only is elocution important but you must also improve your sight-reading, so to do that you must read something different every time. Not much will be achieved by reading the same script over and over again. The advantage of variety is that you get used to discovering words you have never mouthed out loud before. You get used to practising with different styles; you will even learn to make believe the **written** script you are reading was meant to be **spoken**. Of course if the script is written to be spoken it is far easier to read. As a voice you will be confronted with all sorts of styles; you will need to realise quickly what is going on and adapt to that style. The punctuation might not be quite what you expect and might hinder your reading instead of helping it. Beginners find it difficult sometimes to negotiate parentheses, but that can be done by putting a little pause before and after the words in between parentheses. If you read aloud regularly you will develop a knack for reading. Through experience you will find yourself in a position where you are not surprised by anything anymore. Well, there are always new twists and turns you will have never seen before, but their number will diminish with practice.

It is not unusual for a voice to stumble even on a short word and to have to retake it. That happens through stress and for all sorts of other reasons. Your brain might be concerned by something you read in the previous sentence, you are not sure if you read the right word or if it made sense, but you read on because you have been conditioned to carry on regardless. The reason you carry on reading is normal and is due to your training. (I suppose if you have been used to reading the news **live**, then you will find it a bit difficult to stop and restart, but of course it needs to be done for a **recording**.) It takes a little time for your mind to analyse the situation in the background. You then fluff accidentally or decide to stop to check the sentence that concerns you. There is nothing wrong in stopping and telling the studio manager or the director that you would like to listen to the previous sentence or the previous paragraph. You might explain to them that you are not sure about the previous sentence – you don't know at this stage if it is because of the way you read it or if it is something else. You might in fact discover that the reason something is bugging you is because you don't understand the sentence. The thing to do in such a case is to relax (use this opportunity to take a few deep breaths), look at the offending sentence and decide what to do next. If you don't understand it when you read it first time around, there might very well be a problem with the sentence.

The listener will not have a chance to listen back in most instances. If he does not understand, his mind will be distracted and will miss the next few seconds or minutes of the film as well and that is certainly something that has to be avoided at all costs. You therefore need to analyse the situation, either listen to the

English or look at the English script if there is a copy in the studio, or it might be in a column next to your own language, if the script has been well prepared. At that point you might discover that the problem is with the translation, something has been misunderstood by the translator or it might be that the English itself is not very clear. In this case you ask the director what is meant by that sentence. You are then in a position to modify the script so that it makes sense with the picture. I have added "with the picture", because it might very well be that the translator did not understand the script because the film was not provided.

Once you see the picture, it very often becomes very clear what the words should say. (I also think it is not a very good idea as a voice to do a demolition job on the translation. In my experience it creates an unnecessary tension in the studio. After all the voice does not know the circumstances under which the translation has been done and an undiplomatic reaction could be quite counterproductive. I know I said earlier that I picked up a lot of clients in the early days when the translations did not fit. But I did not have to criticise the translation, clients could see for themselves what the problem was. If they came to the conclusion that the specific problem of length could be addressed by asking the voice to do the translation, well, that was fine by me.) If you are an English voice, the problem might be that the original script itself is not quite right. Do not hesitate to suggest tactfully an alternative to what is written on the page in front of you.

It might also be that you just fluffed the words or that you felt your elocution or intonation was not quite clear enough; in such a case you might just want to ask to retake the sentence or the paragraph straight away, which is sometimes faster than listening, and then deciding if it is acceptable or not. So the fact that your brain is engaged in analysing a worry might very well make you trip up on an easy word a couple of seconds later. However, you will sometimes stumble on a long word that will seem difficult to you because you have never used it before, you might not even know what it means. In such a case you could find yourself retaking it half a dozen times, getting hot under the collar, getting nervous and unsure of yourself. Well, I cannot repeat it often enough, take stock, relax and take a few deep breaths. In other words, do not panic. It happens to everybody and as long as it does not happen all the time you are all right.

One way to try to avoid getting stuck on a word is to stop, look at the word and its structure and maybe put some marks on the different syllables with your pencil so that it becomes a series of five or six short words. This way the word becomes easier to negotiate. I also use another system with those sorts of words. I might write it by hand in large letters well spaced and I say it to myself aloud, very loud, a few times and I memorise it. When it comes to reading it with the sentence, I hardly look at it and just say it. The problem is that this long word might have so many letters that the message captured by your eyes is not clear, so the idea of using your short term memory to overcome the actual look of the word on the page seems good. It certainly works for me. Sometimes there is a recurring word I find difficult to say. It might not even be an especially difficult word, just something I don't find easy to read. It is quite funny in a way, but when my eyes spot that word, they just skim over it and jump directly to the rest of the sentence and I mouth the word from memory. What really happens is that I am using another part of the brain which is not very busy at that stage to give the reading part a little break.

When you read aloud you must look ahead a bit so that you know what is coming and understand the meaning of the sentence. This seems quite obvious, but it needs to be done as otherwise you might not be able to carry, in your delivery, the right inflection and the right meaning. You have to be careful not to accelerate your delivery when you do that! It has a tendency to happen and you start reading faster and faster. Of course this is not surprising at all; we all try to read faster and faster all the time to take in as much information as we can from the numerous documents we receive every day on our desks. To read for a voice-over you must unlearn all these techniques you have toiled upon to read faster.

To be able to read for more than a few seconds at a time you must be able to control your breathing. It is not because you are reading that you must stop breathing! The first thing to bear in mind is that you need to breathe through the nose. Knowing the diaphragmatic breathing technique, which is the one used by all actors, is fundamental. It's true that in voice-over recordings you will not be asked to project your voice as on stage, but still if you want your voice to have a "body" and not to sound too feeble, you must support it with air coming not from your throat (or you'll lose your voice in one session) but from your belly. A "rich", vibrant voice is a voice always supported by correct breathing. If you breathe through your mouth you are in danger of drying your throat and producing a croaking noise, dare I say it, like a *frog*!

A glass of water by your side might be useful if your throat dries up. You will always be offered a drink when you arrive at a studio and if for some reason this is overlooked do not hesitate to ask for a glass of water. Tea can sometimes cause problems. The film on the top of the cup that you can see every now and again could get stuck to your vocal cords and stop you from reading; this happened to me once and I have never drunk a cup of tea in a studio ever since! On the other hand, some voices swear by using milky coffee and use it to lubricate the organ! Professional voice coaches do **not** recommend consuming any dairy products before a session. I have noticed that an increasing number of people are drinking herbal teas in studios. Studios are becoming aware of this new development and more and more of them offer a selection of herbal teas.

But back to breathing. So, you inhale through your nose and you breathe out through your mouth. You actually begin speaking once you have started to breathe out, which is what happens naturally when you speak without thinking about it. However, when reading, you need to become conscious of your breathing by finding the appropriate place to breathe in the sentences. Full stops are of course designed for that very purpose, but some sentences are very long and you need to find other places to do it. With practice you will know where to do it and how deep you can breathe. As a rule of thumb, you have more time at a full stop and therefore you can breathe deeper than at a comma for example. You should not hesitate to mark your script; this will certainly help you at the beginning of your career, as it will serve as a larger visual reminder of the places you need to breathe, larger that is than the traditional punctuation.

It is always a good idea to breathe very deeply a few times before you start the recording: it gives you plenty of oxygen to start your reading, but it also helps you relax. So shoulders back, chest out and breathe deeply through the nose. The oxygen goes down into your lower abdomen...well, after all I have had three children and attended pre-natal clinics, so no wonder I know how to breathe!!! Joking apart, this is very important. It is also very good if you can avoid making a lot of noise when you are inhaling; if you do, make sure that it is controlled and that you stop the noise for a fraction of a second before you start speaking, this way the sound engineer can cut the breath out if the client wants to. It is especially important in the case of a training course or a language course, when the students might listen again and again to the same sentences. If there is a soundtrack with M&E, Music and Effects, some of the breathing might be hidden, but that rarely happens for the type of recording I have just mentioned. A lot of heavy breathing may be quite disturbing. To find out about the amount of noise you emit while breathing, you could ask the sound engineer to show you the wave file recorded on the computer.

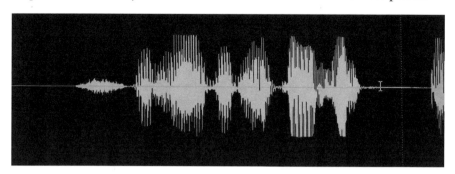

Picture of a sound wave: this is quite a normal-looking sound wave. The voice goes up and down, but you can probably see right at the beginning an oblong form looking like a rugby ball. It is obviously some sound, but it does not look quite normal. It is in fact an intake of air.

With time you will hopefully be able to breathe deeply without making much noise. However, you might hear on the radio, for example, some people who inhale very loudly before each sentence. That could be due to the poor respiratory technique of the speaker. Alexander[2] developed a technique which allowed him not only to breathe effortlessly but also noiselessly. However, the noise can also be emphasised by the type of microphone, the distance at which it is positioned from the mouth and the experience of the engineer.

I have mentioned earlier the setting of levels by the studio manager and yourself when you first sit in front of the mic. This might also involve the studio manager coming into the sound cubicle (also called "booth" in American English), and moving the microphone. That might happen a couple of times depending again on the circumstances on the day, the experience of the engineer and your own experience.

All these activities are quite normal and part of the recording session. Very rarely will the engineer ask you to touch anything in the studio, to move the mic or something like that; they might ask you to lean in more or to go back a fraction. I should emphasise that it is quite important to remain at the same distance from the microphone during the entire recording. Some voices, because of their own nature, have a tendency to be more agitated than others in the studio. They might lean forward to emphasise a point, but this is to be avoided. We see politicians doing it more in certain countries than in others when they lean on the lectern or bang their fists on it. It goes without saying that all these activities are taboo in a studio environment!

Having said that, I have seen a couple of colleagues gesturing around in studios. It is quite funny really because they know it could make some noise, so they wave their arms, but as far away from themselves as they normally would. Of course they have to be conscious of not touching anything! That is not always easy as some studios are quite small, with a lot of things crammed in which look like clutter to the untrained eye but are vital, like microphone stands, cables, lectern, table lamp, cup of drinks, water jug and so on!

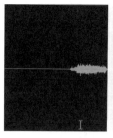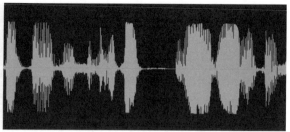

In this picture you can see, highlighted, the space between the intake of air and the start of the speech per se. This space is very large and makes it very easy for the engineer to take the breath out. The breath could still be cut out if the space was much smaller, as long as there is a space.

The vertical line shows where the studio manager can cut the file.

The reader in this example is very well known and has many years of experience. His voice is highly recognisable in his home country and he works as a radio announcer as well as a voice for corporate productions. He is very professional, does not mess about in the studio, does not fluff, but he is a heavy breather. However, he is easy to edit, because…he knows how to control the timing of his breathing. I have known him for thirty years and he still smokes, less than in the past, but he still does and that probably has an impact on his breathing. Another colleague who was also very good as a voice gave up smoking when he realised how heavy his breathing had become and that he was going to start losing work because of it!

In this picture you can see the "breath" highlighted. It is not very pleasant to the ear to have to listen to that level of breathing, because of course if it happens at the beginning of the sentence at that level it tends to happen as well inside the sentence, albeit at a lesser level.

The highlighted part is the sound made by the breath.

Once the engineer has taken out the breath it looks like this. This is time-consuming for the engineer and therefore costs more money to the client.

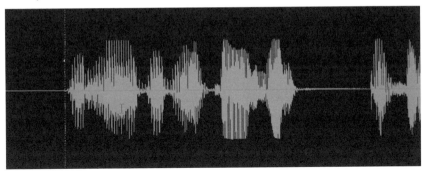

Here the breath has been cut out.

Mind you, in the old days, the editing was done with a razorblade and the magnetic tape was physically cut and then glued together again with a sticky tape and it was even more time-consuming.

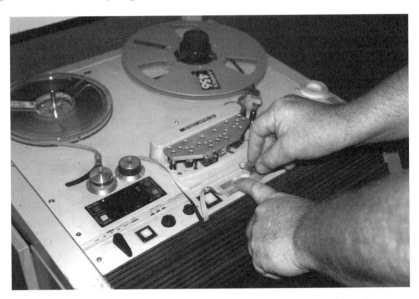

Editing by hand with a razor blade on a reel-to-reel machine.

I remember spending a night editing the first English person I interviewed in French. His French was grammatically correct but he had not practised for many years and paused between almost every word. To be able to use a minute and a half of the interview

I had to cut out all the empty spaces. When he heard the broadcast he was absolutely delighted with his French, but I never interviewed him again!

Now, to improve your reading, there are a number of little tricks you could use, as articulation is essential. Before starting anything, practise opening your mouth as much as you can while reading, really articulating every single vowel. If you look at yourself in the mirror, you'll find that even when you think your mouth is wide open, it actually isn't. To improve your elocution and articulation for example, you could try reading with a pencil in your mouth, it is a little disconcerting at the beginning but it is a very useful exercise. This way you have to concentrate on using your lips and your tongue to emit the right sound, or as close as possible to the right sound.

There are two types of exercises here. One is to put the pencil across and gradually push it back and the other one is to put it straight and again push it back so that it becomes a real obstacle to your tongue. Please do not push so far back that you are going to be sick all over your desk! I think the pictures illustrate this technique quite well.

Not only will you start reading very clearly once you have taken the pencil out of your mouth but it will also help you get rid of your regional accent if you so wish. I have used it to improve my English but not to the point of losing my French accent. I still do a number of recordings and interviews on the strength of this accent, so I don't want to lose it altogether. But I remember very well when I went for an audition almost thirty years ago at the BBC and the director told me he loved my voice but that my accent was too strong and the listeners would not understand me. Within a short while I was able to tone it down enough to start doing recordings in English! So it does work. It is of course much easier to improve your reading in your native tongue than in a foreign one. To help you salivate and again to acquire more dexterity with your tongue you could put a couple of pebbles in your mouth. Nothing new here! You might remember Demosthenes, the Greek philosopher who had a stutter and improved his diction dramatically by speaking to his students with small stones in his mouth while walking along a beach where the waves were making a lot of noise as well!

To improve your articulation you will need to practise some word strings. These of course will depend on the language you are using. A voice coach will tell you which ones to use and how often and how fast you need to read them. Reading tongue twisters in any language is a very good exercise; it can also be entertaining for your friends, as you'll be able to show off if you have practised well, whereas they will make a dog's dinner of it. Here is an example in English that is given sometimes by voice coaches:

"She stood upon the balustraded balcony, inexplicably mimicking him hiccoughing and amicably welcoming him in!"

And there are some very nice ones in other languages like this one in French:

"Les chaussettes de l'archiduchesse sont-elles sèches, archi-sèches?"

In German there is the classic:

"Fischers Fritz fischt frische Fische, frische Fische fischt Fischers Fritz."

In Mandarin we have the following one with the phonetics to give you an idea of the problem — and in addition there is the added difficulty of the four tones:

門外有四十四隻獅子，
men wai you si shi si zhi shi zi
不知是四十四隻死獅子？
bu zhi shi si shi si zhi si shi zi
還是四十四隻石獅子？
hai shi si shi si zhi shi shi zi

And a couple of examples in Polish:

W Szczebrzeszynie chrząszcz brzmi w trzcinie.
(In Szczebrzeszyn the beetle makes sounds in the reeds.)

Stół z powyłamywanymi nogami.
(a table with broken legs)

Mind you I am a little bit like a Polish table when it comes to it; I do not have a leg to stand on. For me Polish is always a tongue twister!

Some voices have at the beginning of their career a projection problem, in other words they either do not speak loud enough or they shout. Projecting properly is the art of sounding louder without shouting. There is the stage example of the actor who is speaking to the audience or to another actor without the other characters on the stage supposedly hearing what he is saying; he does what is known in the theatre as an aside. He can be heard in the rafters but he is not shouting and the spectators believe the other actors on stage cannot hear what he is saying. Projection is therefore very important and must be *practised* so that there is enough level for the engineer to make a good recording. You do not need to be as good as a stage actor doing an aside, but you need to be able to control the volume of your voice to make a good recording. Look at people using their mobile phones and you will notice that some are heard miles away and you wonder why they are using a phone at all as everyone in the entire train can hear them, but others have a very serious talk sitting next to you and you need to concentrate very hard to overhear what they are saying. I am not saying that you should listen in to private conversations, of course!!!

To achieve good projection and a good read in general it is highly recommended that you sit up. I am not asking you to stand up, even though it would probably produce a better recording if you were. When recording plays or language courses we very often stand up around the microphones, as it makes it easier to act. Rest assured that you will not be asked to record six hours of voice-over material standing up. Even if you are sitting, it is important to adopt a good position, it will help you with your breathing and therefore your entire performance will sound better. It is important to speak directly into the microphone rather than into the table. To achieve this you might find it easier to hold your page next to the microphone with one hand. In some studios you

have the choice of using a lectern or something more rudimentary and much cheaper called a "book chair" that does the trick very well.

In this picture you can see the script on the Book Chair. You can just about see that there are two columns and that the paragraphs are the

same sizes. The third column has titles that appear on the screen. You will also notice that there are no shadows on the script as the light has been positioned in such a way that there is nothing between the light source and the script.

If you speak into the table, your voice will bounce back into the microphone or part of it will be absorbed by the material covering the table, and this is not conducive to a good recording. Some people do get away with speaking into the table, but it is not ideal and not encouraged if we want to maintain the high standards of recordings achieved in the United Kingdom. Some people get away with it because the studio manager or the director cannot hear the difference or are not bothered, but it does not mean it is a good thing to do.

You will also very likely be confronted with pops at one stage or another. Popping is a jargon word. It is caused by an undue amount of air coming out of your mouth and hitting the microphone membrane too loudly. The studio manager will stop you and ask you to redo a sentence because you popped on a word. It is very often in fact happening on one letter. The best candidate for popping is the letter "p", but any explosive consonants will do it. This happens more in some languages than others. There are a number of ways to avoid popping. The first one as far as the voice is concerned is to be in total control of the projection. Even so, you might find that you are suddenly popping when it has never happened to you before! That might be caused by the set-up and the equipment in the studio. The microphone might be more sensitive to pops than some others you have used. You might be closer to the mic than usual, so moving away a bit might cure the problem; you might need to speak very slightly to the side of the microphone rather that directly into it, without of course sounding "off". You will be helped in most instances by the SM who might come into the cubicle and change the mic position. You will find that in most studios there is a little screen in front of the mic. These screens have been especially designed to reduce the amount of popping, but there might still be some popping going through. I say especially designed but I remember in the early days a studio where the engineer had used some of his wife's tights to create a diffusing screen which worked extremely well. A way to stop it happening is always found on the day – it has to be. The recording would not be usable if there were pops in it as they cannot be removed after the event!

Speed of delivery

You will also need to work on the speed of your delivery. You will have to know what speed is acceptable for delivery in your own language. This does vary considerably according to the language. Italian and Spanish can be read pretty fast. I remember an instance of an Italian newsreader on the RAI, a lady who was well known for the high speed of her delivery. I don't think it was that good, but it had become her "trademark" and was acceptable from her; because of course her diction was also superb as otherwise she would not have been understood at all. Spanish news can be read pretty fast, but some of the documentaries I have watched on Spanish television have superbly spoken narrations. So depending on the subject matter and of course the language, there might be different speeds of delivery; this will be dictated by tradition, local culture and the like. As I mentioned before, you very often will be directing yourself, so you will need to know what the ideal speed of delivery is for a given subject. The reason you will need to know is that many directors don't know your language and to their ears, whatever the speed you are reading at will always be *too* fast. You will therefore need to explain that, listening back, you are convinced that the speed is right for the intended audience.

However, there are directors who will insist on making you read slower. Well, as every one knows, "the client is always right!" Once you know yourself what the speed should be, you will have to be able to vary the delivery of your speech. There are a number of reasons you should be able to do that. Different scripts will require different speeds. Different directors will also require different speeds, but there are also the problems produced by the time constraints I have told you so much about earlier. You might have to make a sentence fit by accelerating the delivery or slowing it down. When you hit a problematic area in the film like that, you might have to do a few retakes until it fits, and then you will need to listen back to it to make sure it does not sound ridiculous one way or the other. With experience, you will be able to judge very quickly if you can make the script fit or if you need to cut out some words, add a few or rewrite the sentence all together. You will need to practise varying the speed of your delivery while you are training yourself. Sometimes you will read very fast, too fast in fact, but that is a good exercise and at other times you will read very slowly and then you will practise going from one speed to the other in the same sentence. Then back to a normal delivery, with some sentences a bit faster if there is a sense of urgency and then slower if the mood becomes dramatic for example.

Of course, whatever the speed, the elocution must still be one hundred per cent. Now, I suppose I was lucky in training myself to vary the speed of my reading when I was working at the BBC. In the mornings for example we had a slot which ended at 7h29mn and 28 seconds. There was then a network break and the next transmission in another language started four seconds later. The way we used to do it was to start a music tape two or three minutes to the second before the end of our transmission time, so that the last note of music would be played on the last second of transmission. The challenge for me was to try not to use the music and speak to the ultimate second. I think I was pretty good at judging the speed of my delivery in the last minutes to make sure I would finish speaking on the dot at twenty-eight seconds past. I was helped in that by an old-fashioned clock with a hand marking the seconds. I must say that this trick of being able to control my delivery speed was very useful in my subsequent career as a voice-over. It helped me hit key words or actions on the screen. All these skills cannot be improvised, but they can be acquired with practice.

Speaking one language while listening to another

Another aspect of your training which you must not forget is the ability to listen to one language and speak in another. This is still very often the way we record our voice-overs in foreign languages. Our English colleagues have it a bit easier here as they work most of the time on the original versions and therefore only to picture. Having said that, they sometimes have to listen to a guide track which has been recorded in English by the director or someone in the office to give them a rough idea of the pace of the film; this means a rough cut of the film can be made before the final edit with the voice of the professional reader. (It probably shows my age that I still refer to "rough cut of the film" when, I suppose I should say "rough edit of the video!") The script has been specifically written for them and the rough recording means that the narration should fit properly to the pictures. If the foreign voice needs to **listen and speak**, I would say that for the English voice in many instances it is more **look and speak.** This also requires quite a talent as you need to read from your script and at the same time keep an eye on the screen.

I suggest the first thing you should try to do, to have a feel for what I am trying to explain, is to listen to the radio and simply repeat what the speaker is saying. At this stage I don't think it is necessary to record yourself. You will know when you cannot keep up any longer with the speaker or when you start to make too many mistakes. Check how long you can keep your concentration doing that. When you can do that sort of exercise reasonably well for ten or fifteen minutes you can then start practising for the real thing. You will have to create the right environment to do so. There are a number of options. If you have a tape recorder you could start playing a sound track in English (I am saying "English" as most of the work done in the UK originates in English, but the same rules apply if you record from other languages. I have indeed followed guide tracks in languages I can't really understand – it will become clear why that can be done a bit later), and record your version in your own language. To do this type of exercise successfully you require a player as well as a pair of cans. The hard bit, of course, is that to do your training, you might have to translate scripts yourself. Mind you, this is quite a good exercise in translating for the spoken word. (Remember I am not trying to sell a language course using spurious claims like: *"learn a language in three days!"* I said right from the start that it is not easy, but the rewards can be good.) You then will be able to listen to yourself. Depending on your IT skills and equipment you might find it easier to use your computer or a combination of both a cassette player (to play the original) and the computer (to record your own voice). You can use a cheap microphone to do the recording on your computer and if you are using one of the latest Windows platforms you will probably have some sound recording software good enough for the purpose of your exercises. Longer term you could of course think about getting your own home studio (I will tell you more about this in a little while). To be able to read well while listening to another language you must operate a sort of selective listening. In other words you should not listen to the whole script; you should concentrate on the start of the sentences, on pauses in the sentences and maybe on key words, and on the end of sentences. You might be able to start breathing roughly the same way as the original reader, and, without realising it, start practising for phrase synch while doing your voice-overs. At the risk of repeating myself, your work as a voice will be made easier if the translation is well done, if the sentence rhythm has been respected and of course if the length is the same.

Once you have made your first test you must analyse it. You should listen for the way you delivered the script. You must ask yourself a number of questions: "Do I sound confident? Do I sound authoritative?" Authoritative, *yes,* but you don't want to sound aggressive or threatening. You must also look at the number of fluffs you made. If you have made too many, you need to do more sight-reading, without the added difficulty of listening to the guide track. A few weeks later, you might do another test to assess your progress. At this early stage I don't think you should worry too much about the length. The important factor is that you should practise listening to one language while speaking in another.

There is another very important factor to take into consideration, and that is just as valid for any translator. I would strongly recommend that you keep in touch with the spoken language of your country. It might seem quite obvious and you might not see the danger when you first move to your new country. So there are a number of ways to keep up-to-date with your native language. You might be in a family environment which allows you to speak your mother tongue every day and that is a good start. You might have around you a large community speaking your language. In Ealing, in West London, we have for example a large number of Polish people and they do speak Polish every day. They meet their compatriots on a regular basis and have managed to preserve their culture and language. We have neighbours whose children are third generation Polish and still speak the language beautifully. But that might not be quite enough, however. Before 1990, it was not very easy for Polish people to go back home, it was very difficult if not impossible for them to listen to a Polish radio station and of course there were no televisions. So Adam, my neighbour, told me of his problems in Warsaw. His Polish was very good, he did not have a foreign accent and thought he would have absolutely no problems getting by in the capital, but people looked at him in a very strange way, for example, when he asked them in perfect Polish how to buy a train ticket. A foreigner would not have had any problems, but how could a Polish grown-up be so ignorant as to not be able to perform such a mundane task? So he had to explain every time where he came from and why he could speak Polish so well. He also realised that he was speaking quite an old-fashioned style of the language. He could have been ninety instead of forty! It took me a little while to understand why Polish people in the UK remained Polish and preserved their identity completely through many generations whereas in France for example, they became French very quickly. When the Poles came to Britain, an Anglican country, they found they did not have a Catholic church around the corner with a large congregation. They therefore either became the majority in the local Catholic church if there was one, or they had to create their own, and this is how they remained Polish. In France each village has a Catholic church and therefore the Poles just joined in and became part of the flock, feeling French very quickly.[3] This sort of environment is of course very useful for a translator, but it is not enough to keep up with living languages, as new words come in every day and the way of speaking changes all the time. You would probably recognise the delivery of a newsreader in the '50s and hear how different it is today. I remember voicing some Pathé News Reels of that period in the '80s. The originals were in English and I reproduced the equivalent French style. It was relatively easy for me as I had been brought up at that time and listened to the radio quite often even then. Of course, going back to your own country is ideal but that is not always practical, for all sorts of reasons. It might be too expensive, it might be too far or it might not be possible at all.

When I worked in Bush House (the home of the BBC World Service) during the Cold War, numerous colleagues could not go back home. Some of them used a different name for fear their family behind the Iron Curtain would be persecuted. I have noticed, and I am sure many of you have noticed the same thing, that in a small community it is very difficult to keep the language at the same level as in the home country. The vocabulary shrinks every year. I remember well when I was in Bush House that when a new colleague was recruited it was like a breath of fresh air coming into the Service, but after a few months, it had gone. It was quite astonishing to hear "new" words. It was not even that the words were new; it was just that in our small group we had sort of forgotten to use them. Over the years, that can have an arthritic effect. Not only does the vocabulary shrink but more and more English words come into everyday conversations. It is quite natural as there are so many typically English things that cannot easily be translated; the translation will be an equivalent and it is so much easier to use the English word. I am trying to learn a little bit of Greek at the moment so I listen to LGR, the London Greek Radio; it feels good, because there are quite a number of English words thrown in that Greek people in Greece would not understand but that everyone here takes for granted. I am not singling out the Greeks for being sloppy, we all do it. I have heard it on the Italian Radio in London and on some of the Asian channels as well.

A discipline I have imposed on myself is to listen to a French radio station every day. Mind you, it makes me quite upset when I hear all the English words being used by the French; very often it does not enrich the language, it bastardises it. I am not at all against foreign words being used in another language as that can be quite enriching when these words bring with them a full concept or have a historical relevance. In the '80s for example we all enriched our knowledge of Russian with the words *Perestroika* and *Glasnost*. Of course the equivalents exist in other languages, but their use even today means we are referring to that historical period and to the turmoil the USSR was going through. There are countless numbers of words that come into the language, and they are called borrowed words. For example in English and many different languages the word "Première" is used (not always spelt with the accent) to mean the opening night of a show. "Première" means simply "first" in the feminine in French. Well, every language must have a word for "first" but when the French word is used, everyone knows what is meant by it. Why is a French word used for that? Well, it probably has to do with the dominance of the French language in literature, in the arts in general and in diplomacy over many centuries.

Nowadays, it is the turn of the English/American language to be dominant and to have many words borrowed by other languages. The Germans, for example, love to use English words. Even if they don't speak the language, they go as far as **inventing** English words like a *handy*, used instead of *mobile phone* or *cell phone*. When we talk about *Franglais*, my English friends almost always come up with the word "week-end"[4] that has become French. This is a good example of a word being introduced in another language. The reason is simple; traditionally in France we do not have a weekend. Most people work on Saturday morning or even all of Saturday. As a teenager in France I went to college every Saturday, all day. To compensate for it we had a day off in the middle of the week – on Thursdays which was then changed to Wednesdays in the second half of the twentieth century.[5] The French Canadians have made up an expression for "weekend", simply *"fin de semaine"* but the reasoning behind it is that the French language in that little corner of North America was much more threatened by American English than it is in France, or at least that was certainly the case in the '60s and '70s where it could have disappeared if serious remedial measures had not been taken.[6] The situation has improved tremendously since then and it looks like French is going to survive in Quebec.

For a translator based in the UK, it becomes very difficult to know which words to translate and which words to keep in English. I remember a voice-over script where only one word had been changed by the client back in Germany; it was the word *Gruppe* which had been changed to *team*! No prizes for guessing what the original English was! (*Gruppe* of course is the correct translation of *team* but *team* is more fashionable.) There are times in history when strong governments as Italy and Germany had in the '20s and '30s forbade the usage of foreign words. Mussolini went as far as changing the word *Standard* which was the name of a department store to *Standa* to make it sound Italian, but the concept was American and the Italianised name did not change that. French governments have tried to do the same sort of thing, but of course you cannot dictate the way people speak, so the aim of the French authorities was to force the civil servants to use "French" words. It does not seem to work that well. Just one example of this nonsense: a national company is called "France Telecom". Well, the syntax is wrong, it should be "*Telecom Française*".

I would like to take another example from France. It is all very well for a singer called Lorie to invert the word order in a *Chanson* called *La Positive Attitude*[7] but when M Jean-Pierre Raffarin, the French Prime Minister at the time used the expression it did show that legislation does not work to control the way a language evolves. In the case of *la positive attitude*, the words are French as well as English, but the syntax is English. In proper French he should have said: *l'attitude positive*. However, by changing the word order in this manner, he not only showed that he was in touch with a popular singer and her followers, but also managed to give much more strength to his message. Nobody would have taken much notice if he had simply said that people should adopt *une attitude positive* to solve their problems. To me this is the equivalent of Norman Tebbit (then chairman of the Conservative Party) who said his father, when unemployed, did not sit around but got on his bike and looked for a job. The change in the word order put an incredible emphasis on what he was saying. However, the result is that now I hear everybody putting the adjective before the noun! Soon, no one will know what the "correct" French should be, the language will have moved on and nobody can do anything much about it. And there are other examples where the popular usage of the wrong preposition has been picked up by the mass media like *La bande à Bonnot*. It should be *de* instead of *à*. In 1911–1912 when this group of nihilists made the headlines, their own popular language was used by the media. It is used now very often on national radio and television stations with very few people realizing that they are making an historical reference to an event which is totally irrelevant to what they are talking about. I have mentioned only a few examples, but I think this is enough to show that it is not possible to use legislation to influence the way people speak. It seems to me that this type of legislation is used as a smoke screen to hide the incompetence of the Education Department. If French kids were taught French well enough in the first place, they would know which words are French and which ones are foreign and would not have any problems finding the right word to express the right idea; they would know what the French syntax is and not use the English one. It is far easier to pass a law which is not going to be enforceable than to reform the education system! Sorry, another of my digressions!

Therefore to keep up-to-date with your language as it is spoken I would strongly recommend that you listen to the radio every day. If your language is not broadcast on long wave you will not be able to listen to it on the radio. A few years ago you would have had to resort to listening to short wave radio. Short waves travel around the world but the reception is not very good and it is quite an art in itself to listen to this type of broadcast. Short waves travel best at night so you might have had to listen to your broadcast in the middle of the night. However, today we can listen to radio stations on the Internet. Admittedly it is much easier if you are on Broadband (also known as ADSL or DSL). Lately more and more broadcasters are letting listeners tune in to the programming live or to any programmes during the seven days following the broadcast; this is absolutely wonderful as you do not have to listen to your favourite programme when it just happens to be broadcast at three in the morning. There are therefore no more excuses not to keep abreast of what is going on back home and also, of course, of the evolution of your language.

Reading newspapers and magazines as well as contemporary novels was always a way to keep in touch with the language, but if I have insisted on the radio it is because in the context of our specific work as voices, the spoken language is more important than the written one.

Speaking to camera

Now that you have become proficient at sight reading you might want to take your career another step forward. You might indeed be asked by your clients to work in front of the camera rather than behind the microphone. I am not talking here about becoming an actor or an actress but reading a piece to camera convincingly.

Suddenly another factor comes into the equation when you are asked to speak in front of the camera: it is your appearance. The way you dress will of course very much depend on the client's requirements. It is generally a sort of business-like attire that will be required, with little make-up if any.

Another difficulty will be added by the larger number of people involved in the production of the film. As well as the director, a representative from the client might be there, the cameraman will be helped by a sound engineer and you might also have someone dealing with the lights. The sound engineer will probably put a lapel mic on to you and ask you to pull the wire through some of your clothing. This is quite normal procedure and you should be prepared to have people coming very close to your comfort zone, though it should not last more than a few seconds. The lights might be a little disturbing to start with and you will need to acclimatise yourself as it might affect your eyes. If it still does it after a little while, you should mention it to the film director or the cameraman or the person in charge of lighting. You need to be comfortable to read. As well as the lapel mic, there might be a boom mic on a long perch, coming up and down. The reason I am mentioning all these things is that they will considerably change the studio environment you are used to working in. The film studio tends to be much larger than the cubicle of a sound studio where you can feel very cosy. The film studio can be noisy between takes; it is very often too hot or too cold. There is a lot of seemingly lost time as everyone needs to be ready before you start reading. The lights will need to be adjusted so that there are no shadows falling in the wrong places and so on. The process is still pretty fast compared to what takes place for a feature film where many actors interact and move around. Here you are sitting and probably not going to be asked to move much. Maybe every now and again the director might decide to change the camera angle and reposition you so that you will have to turn your head to the right or to the left, or maybe stand up if you were sitting or sit down if you were standing up.

You might be wondering about the reading, indeed you will not use the piece of paper you have become accustomed to read from. You will have to become acquainted with a piece of equipment called an *auto-prompt* or *Autocue, prompt*[8] for short. The prompt is made up of a piece of glass poised at an angle in front of the camera lens. The camera can see through the glass without registering the words running on it. The words are projected to the glass which is being used as a screen by a projector situated at the bottom of the camera. The prompt operator will be sitting in

front of a computer in the background. This Autocue, shown on the left, is one of the latest used in television newsroom.

An important part of your work will depend on your own preparatory work with the auto-prompt operator. Working in a foreign language, you are going to be confronted with an operator who might not speak your language, and that is a difficulty that is not easy to resolve. The first thing to do is to make sure that you revise the script that has been input to the computer to make sure there are no typos or errors, as that would very likely make you fluff. In the past it was a struggle as the files used by the prompters were not compatible with the ones generated by the translators. The entire script had to be keyed in by the prompt operator who, as I said, might not have been very fluent in the language, in any case very rarely a native speaker of your language. It meant that there were many mistakes; sometimes the software did not support accents which meant the sight reading was even more difficult for languages like French. You can imagine the difficulties with Arabic, Japanese or Korean for example. On some of the more primitive systems it was not possible to make any corrections on site. It was therefore necessary to rehearse and be prepared for the mistakes and try to use your memory to cope with the added difficulty. Nowadays, the compatibility is perfect between the different software, thus making it possible to amend the script "on the fly" the same way as you might change your script in a recording studio; in fact it is even better because you don't do it by hand but via a keyboard.

Retakes could be a problem so you need to be able to read without fluffing for quite a long time. Here again the director will know when you will be in vision and when images will be superimposed on you. Once out of vision, it is easy to edit or restart. Having said that, it is a "nice to have" for the director if you can read long parts of the script without interruption, as it will give him added opportunities at the editing stages. Your performance will also be affected by the prompt operator; the danger is that the operator might lose the place on the script where you are and not know how fast to make the script scroll in front of your eyes. It is therefore a good idea to try to rehearse quietly with the prompt operator while the other technicians are getting the set ready. You might also lose your way on the script. It happens to everyone: your mind might be distracted and in this environment it might happen even more than in a sound studio. It is not a drama, you only need to stop and restart. If you feel the speed is too fast or too slow you must tell the director as soon as you notice it. Nowadays the speed can be pre-selected and should remain constant throughout, but that is not necessarily ideal as you might want to vary your speed for artistic reasons and also not to sound boring. It is well worth spending a little time setting up the right speed for your style of delivery. It is a little bit like the time spent in the sound studio to set the levels right. In the early days, the operator had to follow you and it was very often a bit of a struggle. You might be trying to catch up or the operator might be trying to catch up with you! It works best when the operator can follow well what you are reading and adjust the speed to your delivery.

Now, in real life you might also be asked to read to camera without auto-prompts. This happens for a number of reasons. The most common one is that the producer has not budgeted for the auto-prompt and the operator which could be quite expensive for a day's work. In my view it is not a real saving because the end product will probably not be as good and it will take longer for the shoot to be completed. This sort of production will probably not have more than a director/cameraman and one assistant doing the sound, the lights and the tea! These types of experiences are not very pleasant, not very professional. I remember doing one like that a few years ago. The script was not sent to me ahead of the session. When I arrived, I discovered the "studio" was a tiny room in a terraced house and indeed there were only two people. The prompts were huge cards with some French written on them. It was OK to read, but there was the problem of the sight-line. The director was quite clever, he did not make us read looking at the camera, or at least not very often and shot most of it from the side. When looking at the camera, the boards cannot be put in front of the lens, so they must be over or under it, or on one side or the other. It really means you need to memorize the lines concerned, otherwise you will be looking at the camera with your eyes wandering away all the time! Not very good! The end results were not very good, and I was not surprised when the director "retired" very soon afterwards. He must have been cheap to the client, but the client realised belatedly that he got what he had paid for!

In this job you must be prepared to face all sorts of unforeseen situations and cope as best as possible on the day. Indeed on the day, your job is to read the script as convincingly as possible, to suggest some changes if there are grammatical mistakes and maybe express some reservations as to the quality of the script, but it is really too late to do much at that stage. If your client did not take more care with the job, I don't think you should upset him in any way. You should be as cooperative as possible. After all, neither you nor I know what the relationship between the film director and the end client is. If the end client has been used to receiving "crap" from that film director and never complained, it might turn out that the film director knows exactly what he is doing. Not making a masterpiece, no, making money! I always try to give my best in any production I am involved in. But I think the secret is never to query something on the day if you do not know the answer. If you are absolutely certain of something, then just suggest to the director that this or that could be changed. Most of the time directors will be delighted if you are helpful, especially if you do it efficiently and without losing time. Some other times, the director will tell you that the script has been approved by the client and that you should not change anything at all. This is fine by me too. If there is something seriously wrong, you will then no doubt be recalled to repair the damage at the cost of the client or the production, not yours!

I have also used another device to help speak to camera when there is no auto-prompt. Auto-prompts tend to be bulky and not easy to carry around if you are filming outside a studio. You might very well be asked to deliver your script while walking down a crowded street or in a park or in any other public place you might imagine, like a factory floor for example as it makes for a much better presentation if the speaker is walking in the environment he or she is talking about. You could be talking about the White Cliffs of Dover while roaming around on top of them or at the bottom. If the script is short you might be able to learn it before the shoot day. I said earlier I did not expect you to do an actor's job, but of course I would encourage you to work as hard as possible to become as qualified at this sort of work as an actor, so in such a situation you could use an *audio-prompt*. I had one made especially for me years ago and I have used it a few times quite successfully. It is similar to the little earpieces television presenters are using. They are using these devices to hear what the person they are interviewing, possibly on the other side of the World, is saying.[9] It is also used by the programme director to give them directions or they are told what the latest piece of news coming up is or that the running order has been changed. During a live interview on the studio floor, they might be asked to come to a conclusion and make sure the interviewee is shutting up in the next five seconds! These technical widgets are linked to the ear by a wire. They do not look very good and they can come out, especially when the presenter or reporter is out in the wild. The type I use is wireless, it has been designed to fit snugly into my own ear, it is not mass produced and it cannot be seen. It is a tiny receiver! It is quite amazing how such a small piece of equipment can be so powerful. Not only does it need to house a receiver but also its own power supply in the shape of a tiny battery. The transmitter can be any type of small tape player. It could be a Dictaphone type of machine, a DAT or a minidisk player. It must be as small as possible so that you can hide it on your body. The aerial transmitting the sound will be connected to the player and could be in the shape of wire going around your neck under your tie. It has to be as close as possible to your head where the receiver is placed. If you are not wearing a tie it will have to be hidden under your shirt or on your back. Ladies will probably have fewer ways to hide the wire, but I leave it to your imagination as to where it could go. You have to familiarize yourself with the hardware. You will need to know how to operate your recorder quickly and efficiently. You are now ready to record the script you will read while the director is listening so that he can tell you how he wants you to deliver the speech. I suggest you record one sequence at the time. You now have the script in its little box and you can hear it inside your ear. Nobody else can hear it and nobody can see the system hidden on your body. "Camera? – Rolling!" "Sound? – Rolling!" "Action!" You press on the play button and you only need to repeat what you hear inside your ear. You will have no problems walking down the road, or pointing at something during the take. If there is a problem, it is easy enough to rewind and start from the top again. Another bonus is that your delivery will always be at the same speed for each take, which might be very useful for the director in the edit suite. Once the first scene has been shot, you start the process again.

If it all sounds too good to be true, well, it is true, but like everything else, you will need to practise using this type of prompt, the same way you learnt to **sight**-read. Once you have acquired your equipment, you will practise regularly recording short passages and then repeating them back. I suggest you start with one minute and increase the length as you become more proficient. You will need a certain amount of concentration to do this exercise. I also suggest that once you start to be able to repeat what you hear for a couple of minutes without too much trouble, you should start to make life a bit more difficult for yourself, by doing something else while repeating the words. The first thing to do is practise walking while talking and little by little increase the difficulty, like opening a door and then maybe going into the kitchen and taking a plate out of a cupboard (I suggest a plastic one, just in case you break your best Wedgwood, I would not like to feel responsible for such a loss). Once you feel confident using this technique you can start telling clients about it.

Only a few people use it, so directors might be a little bit surprised or cautious when you first tell them about it, but once they have seen you in action, they will be thrilled. It means that the shooting can be done much faster and much more efficiently and everybody likes that in business nowadays!

Studio etiquette

Probably the most important thing about studio etiquette is to arrive on time. There are no valid excuses in the eyes of the director for a late arrival. In London people say that the tube did not work; well that is not an excuse, everybody knows the tube is not reliable so extra time should be allocated. The latest I heard was that there was a problem with the ticketing machines, well that is not an excuse either and nowadays travellers can buy an Oyster Card to avoid that problem. I know, I know, after the events of 7th July 2005, there are excuses for being late, but fortunately that sort of situation does not happen very often. The reason I insist on punctuality is that lateness can create very serious problems with considerable costs to the production company. Let's look at the following scenario: the director has decided to record all ten languages the same day, he has booked the voices on the hour every hour one after the other, with the first one arriving at nine o'clock. If the voice arrives ten minutes late and the full hour was needed for the recording to take place, voice number two will probably not be able to start much before twenty past ten and voice number three not before eleven-thirty. We have a nightmare in the making, a financial disaster for the production company. The first voice will not ask for more money, but voice two will very likely ask for an hour and a half, and voice three for two hours, so you can see how high the bill might become for voice ten. It is therefore imperative for voices to arrive on time.

Confronted with such a situation directors need to cut their losses. To achieve that, they need to address the situation very soon. As soon as they realise that voice number two is not catching up on the time it becomes necessary to reschedule the entire day. Voice number three needs to be contacted and if possible asked to come at the end of the day or even the next day. That of course might not be possible for that voice as he or she might already be on the way to the studio, or if contacted in time might not be able to change the time, let alone the day. In such a case then, voice number four must be contacted and rebooked for a later slot. If that is possible, then the time will be made up during that hour and the damage to the production company purse will have been limited. I know as voices this should not really be our concern, but it is because a day that starts badly very often ends in tears. The atmosphere in the studio can become very fraught and instead of enjoying the wonderful experience of recording a good script you find yourself in an unpleasant situation. The director will be sitting on the edge of his seat and become impatient if you make a fluff which normally would have been totally acceptable. After that of course there is the question of the invoices, the situation can degenerate and become pretty ugly which is not conducive to good business relations between all parties concerned. So a ten-minute delay can cause havoc for the other voices as well as for the first one.

So you arrive on time, but you discover that the script you had not seen before is not very good and you over run the session. It is nothing to do with you but it happens. If you have been booked for one hour and if the client has booked the studio for one hour, you might very well be thrown out all together because another client has booked the following hour. However, if we are back to the previous scenario the director needs to apply the same method to limit the damage.

But experienced directors will have had the scripts sent to the voices before the session so that they can assess whether the scripts have been translated by native translators and whether the language is acceptable. Your fee does cover the checking of the script before going into the studio if you have received it. Some companies are very good at sending scripts, some are not. If they take the trouble of making sure the scripts have been sent on time, they expect the voices to read them and check them before arriving in the studio. In fact I remember an event when a client left the company which had been providing him with voices for a number of years and came to us because the Agency was not taking the trouble to pass the scripts on. This was the main reason he left them and came to us. Voices might have a couple of questions on the script to clarify a few points. If they have received the film via Internet or on a VHS they will have been able to check that the length of the translation is not a problem either. Directors might very well want to do that, but for all sorts of reasons they might not be in a position to send you the script before the recording, let alone the video. In such cases directors should, in my opinion (and I have directed quite a number of multilingual sessions) build in "buffers" so as not to be caught by "time's winged chariot".[10]

The first thing to do is estimate the time the script is going to take to be recorded. I would say that a fifteen-minute film should be recorded in about one hour. That should give time for the voice to listen back to the recording and make any corrections if necessary. However, I would ask the second voice to come not one hour later but an hour and a half later, because the first hour can be a bit slower in the studio and the additional thirty minutes might make the session that bit more comfortable. I know as a director, it will cost another half an hour in studio time, but in my view this is money well spent. In any case the time can be used to start editing the session, or making a CD, or doing anything that needs to be done on the recording. After that I would book the voices every seventy-five minutes instead of every hour, just to be sure. If a voice takes a few more minutes then it has no impact on the following session and also most voices will not charge any additional fee for a few more minutes. I would also allow for a lunch break. That is quite useful, not only to re-energize yourself and the SM, but it creates again an additional buffer in case something goes wrong during the morning. I have found that these little buffers make the work really enjoyable for the director, the voices and the studio engineer; they give them a little bit of breathing space they can use to exchange a few words.

It is also quite polite to switch your mobile phone off when you arrive at a studio. Indeed, some of them will ask you to do it as soon as you arrive on the premises. The technical reason is that the wave length of your telephone signal might interfere with some of the recordings in one of the studios, even if you are not recording yourself. It is the same sort of precautionary measure that is taken aboard aircrafts by airline companies. In the cubicle itself, it is quite embarrassing to have the phone ring when you are in full flow. It does happen that an artist forgets to switch it off. I have seen a number of red faces, including mine, and I try never to forget to do it. However, in exceptional circumstances, and I stress "exceptional" if you need to have your phone switched on, then I suggest you ask the SM or the director to keep it for you because a phone call might come in. But there are very few messages that cannot wait for less than one hour before obtaining a reply. Nowadays the message systems on mobile phones are pretty reliable and you should be able to retrieve them at the end of your session and take the necessary measures to call back whoever needs to speak to you. The messaging service works very well all over Europe for telephone users based in the UK. This is quite a new development; it used to be very unreliable until a few years ago, but the big boys seem to have cracked it now.

You should also avoid making any noise once you are inside the cubicle. I covered the respiration problem earlier. I am talking here about noises made by jewellery you might be wearing; even a watch might bang on the table and make a noise that will not necessarily be editable if it happens while you are talking. Most tables in studios are covered with soft material that will absorb the noise, but the rim is made of wood in most instances. A heavy belt buckle could cause a problem; of course it is easy to remove. It is not unusual for men or women to remove some items of jewellery and put them on the table before starting the session. Using a motorbike to go to the recording sessions, I was once caught with my trousers down! The leather was quite heavy and crackly; I said with my trousers down, well that would have been the solution of course, but I could not very well get rid of them! I never stood so still for a recording session in my entire career. A leather jacket is of course not a problem as you can take it off, and there are indeed leather garments that are so soft that they will not cause any problems at all. So beware of what you wear when you go to a recording session. And if you put your jewellery on the table do not forget to put it back on before you leave the studio!

And then there is the noise made by the paper when you turn the page. Experienced translators who read their own scripts will have made sure that paragraphs or sentences do not continue over the page. However, there are many instances when this little measure has not been taken and you must therefore know when the page will have to be turned well in advance. The first technique to master is to make sure that when you turn the page you are not speaking. You can make as much noise as you like when you are not reading as it can be edited easily. If the paper rustle is under your voice, you will have to retake the sentence! With experience and practice you will master the art of preparing a few pages ahead so that you can move from one to the other without making any noise. Remember that you should always be speaking directly into the microphone, so you cannot lay the pages on the entire width of the table, because you would then have to turn your head and you would sound off mic. The SM would hear it after a little while and ask you to retake the offending sentences. Depending on the types of microphone, some will be more forgiving than others; in other words the acceptable angle for the take will be more or less large. The quality of the paper might help. For example the very flimsy type of paper used in the past when carbon copies where made would not be good at all. Heavier paper will help move from one page to the next without making any noise. There is something in the way one holds the paper that is very difficult to describe that must be achieved in order not to make a noise. Hold the paper firmly so that it does not fall out of your hand, but at the same time the fingers must not stick to it as that would make it impossible to move to the next page. So be prepared and if you have to make a noise make sure it occurs when you are not talking. Some voices are very good at doing that and can read ten pages or more without anyone hearing a paper rustle at all; some make a lot of noise and it would be nice if they could master this art – maybe to start playing cards, or something like that might help! However, becoming conscious of the problem will probably solve it in most cases. With our Mediterranean colleagues there is also sometimes the noise produced by hand and arm movements. I must say that I used to wave my arms around when speaking, which is quite normal, being half French half Italian, but I very quickly realised that it was a no-no in a sound recording studio. Sometimes when you are used to emphasising your speech with your hands and you suppress it, something else might happen, like your feet starting to wiggle under the table! Here again, once you become aware of all these things, you can normally control them without too much trouble.

You will also discover that there are many different types of studios and studio cubicles. Some of them will make you feel you are in a spaceship; these tend to be used for very expensive recordings for commercials and are found mainly in Soho, in Central London. Some will be more rudimentary, still very professional but with no frills, and some will be very basic.

You will always have some means of communication with the studio manager and the director. In the worst cases it will be a shout through the door, but that tends to happen less and less. Mind you, I did a recording a few weeks ago in a building where the studio was still being built. I could still smell the glue and the only communication we had was through the door. The cubicle was so small that I had to stand and it was not for a small company either, it was for a TV documentary! Otherwise, you will have an audio link, called talkback with the SM and/or the director. Most of the time they will hear you, but they will have to press a button to give you instructions. You might also have eye contact through a window with double glazing, the two sheets of glass being probably at least thirty centimetres apart to make sure it is absolutely sound proof. In some cases there is no glass partition and you cannot see the people in the control room; that is sometimes the case when the cubicle is far away from the studio, a floor below or above. Some studios will install a television link so that they can see you, some will go as far as having a two-way system so that you can see them as well and some will use only the audio link. You must be adaptable to all the different situations you might encounter. It is sometimes difficult for people who are a bit claustrophobic if there is no glass, and they feel they are really enclosed in a very confined space, like in a lift, really. One charming lady who had this problem when she first came into my cubicle, seems to feel much more relaxed now that she has done it a few times and knows it is quite safe. She did explain her problem and we closed the doors at the last minute to help her overcome it.

Once you have gone a few times to the same studio and you have established a relationship with the SM, you might be in a position where you could ask them to give you a short MP3 of your recording to add to your collection. This is never easy: not only do you need to have the agreement of the client, but the studio manager must also be willing to do this additional work for you. Unless you know them well, it is very difficult to ask for, and even if you do, you might not receive the promised MP3 anyway. Once you have gone, the studio will carry on being very busy and will completely forget about your request and once back in his office so will the director. However, some people will do it. I always feel it is a very good sign that you might have an ongoing relationship developing with them both professionally and personally. It is much easier nowadays than in the past when the voice had to be put on a quarter inch tape, a cassette or a CD. With the advent of MP3 technology, no support is required; no cost of material is involved, only goodwill and a couple of minutes of the SM's time. This is why it has been slightly easier to obtain demos in the past couple of years than previously. But remember, the studio and the client are doing you a favour when they send you an MP3, this is not something that you can take for granted.

Just to recap, the most important thing is to arrive on time; it will make your life easier and your work enjoyable.

---

1   From the *Languages of the World* by Kenneth Katzner, published by Routledge, 3rd Edition.

"Somali is the national language of Somalia, in easternmost Africa. It is spoken by virtually all of the country's seven million people, and by another four million in Ethiopia. Smaller communities exist in Kenya and in Djibouti.

"Somali is one of the Cushitic languages, which form a branch of the Afro-Asiatic family. Following Somalian independence in 1960 two alphabets were selected, from many contenders, for writing the language. One was Roman, the other Osmanian (named after its inventor) which contained elements of both Arabic and Ethiopic scripts. In 1973, however, when Somali was made the country's official language, the government decreed that it would be written in the Roman alphabet."

2   If you are interested in knowing more about adopting a good sitting, or for that matter, standing position, and all the advantages it will bring to your well-being, physical and mental, you might want to get acquainted with The Alexander Technique. See chapter at the end of this book.

3   The sad thing in a way is that their children born in France were French from the start and lost the language and the culture of their parents, but that is what the République is all about. The aim is "integration" and that implies the loss of identity for outsiders coming to settle in France. The Third Republic in the last quarter of the ninetenth century and the first half of the twentieth went even further by wanting to integrate the regions of France. For example in the south of France children were not allowed to speak Provençal in the schoolyard. The same thing was happening with the Basques, the Bretons and so on. The reasoning behind it was political. The government wanted as many French soldiers as possible to fight the next war against its neighbours and therefore tried to develop a very strong nationalist feeling amongst the population.

4   "Weekend": the French spell it with a hyphen! According to Alain Rey in his *Dictionnaire Historique de la langue française* the word came into usage in France in 1906 when referring to the English weekend.

5   The day off on Thursdays was decided at the time of the concordat between the State and the Church in France, at the beginning of the twentieth century. Schooling being compulsory and the State Schools being totally independent from the Church, it was decided that parents would have the opportunity to send their children to study religion on Thursdays at the local church, not on the school premises.

6   Tribute must be paid to Pierre-Eliot Trudeau, the bilingual, bicultural Prime Minister of Canada who tried to make Canada a bilingual country. It has not worked very well in certain provinces, but it certainly allowed Quebec to remain French speaking.

7   « *La positive attitude*
    La positive attitude
    La tête haute
    Les yeux rivés sur le temps
    Et j'apprends, à regarder droit devant
    La positive attitude... »

8   These words all stem from the word "prompter" used in the theatre. According to the OED, the word appeared in 1604: "A person stationed out of sight of the audience, to prompt any actor at a loss in remembering his part."

9   You might ask, but why can they not listen on the loudspeakers like us? Well, that would create what is known as a Larsen effect, this is a howling noise produced by the sound the loudspeakers make when they are too close to a mic. You have probably heard that sort of things at the local jumble sale when the chairperson uses a mic and is positioned in front of the loudspeakers rather than behind them. The earpiece cures this problem.

10 Andrew Marvell, to his coy mistress:

    "But at my back I always hear
    Time's winged Chariot hurrying near..."

HOW I.T.
CAN HELP

Technology has helped both the translators and the voices and will still do it…until it replaces them! Well, in the meantime, let's try to make the most of what is on offer. Technology evolves, replacing the work done by humans, it is inevitable, it only means that we need to retrain constantly to do things that machines cannot do in our place. Last summer I stumbled on a few novels by a French writer called Bernard Clavel who writes books making full use of what I would call "nostalgia". He wrote for example about the changing profession of the mariners working on the Rhône river using horses to pull their barges in *Le seigneur du fleuve*. Their way of life changed dramatically when steam engines started to replace horse-power in the nineteenth century. A few stuck to the horses and died and a new generation took over. In the world of writing, things have also changed tremendously over the centuries. The monks writing books by hand in the Middle Ages lost their jobs when Gutenberg invented printing in the 1450s. The British Library has two copies of the Bibles printed by Gutenberg. (In the UK we have a tendency to associate this invention with Caxton, simply because he was the first one to print books in England in 1476.) There is the example of the mysterious Nemo in Charles Dickens' *Bleak House* (the excellent 2005 television series) who is a scribe and I also remember a novel by the Italian writer Italo Svevo[1] in which the job of the main character was to write. I am not saying he was an author; no, he was more like a calligrapher, he worked for a bank and had to make copies of letters sent to clients, it was just before the typewriter and carbon paper were invented. His job evolved and the scribe became a typist; this job is on the way out as people can type directly into their own computers and, if they are not professional typists, they can use dictating software. I am not even talking about recording your letter on a small "Dictaphone" and then having it typed by a typist, no, I am talking about the software that you can install in your computer and that you can "train" to type your scripts for you. There are numerous software programs that have been designed for that purpose. They have been extensively reviewed in the ITI Bulletins (for readers who are not translators, the ITI is the Institute of Translation and Interpreting) over the past few years. So jobs do change and are replaced by others. Professional life is a never-ending challenge! In today's world we all have to cope with computers whether we like it or not. This trend started in the early '80s and I know of a number of translators who stuck to their guns, they did not want to use a computer when they were already very fast with a typewriter. I know of a case when a translator with forty years' experience waited until clients were desperately asking for files to move on to use a computer, but then came modems and the Internet and again this translator refused for too long to get e-mail. By the time she subscribed she had lost all her clients! I also remember a conversation with a technical translator who was a well known specialist in his field. He was still doing translations long hand in the '90s and managed to survive so long because nobody else could do his type of translation, but even that was not enough. He fought a rearguard action but had to acquire a computer before it developed into a rout!

Computers

As translators we can make use of dictating software if we are not too good at typing, but there are other programs which are potentially much more interesting as they have been specifically designed to assist translators. These programs can work well for repetitive work. For example it is very useful in the pharmaceutical industry where you have to re-enter long lists of formulas. However, to make use of this type of software you also need to make sure that the original writer knows about it and always uses the same words to mean the same things. It works reasonably well with very technical scripts, but of course the translator will still need to edit the resulting script thoroughly. As we can see here again the job is evolving, the technical translator slowly becoming an editor rather than a translator. I personally think this is an improvement as the most painful part of the translator's job is probably typing the translation into the computer and if most of it can be done by a machine, so much the better.

To translate

In the film industry and when you translate the type of material produced to be spoken, the writers try very often to be creative, witty or funny. They try to play on words and that means that the translating software is not usable. The computer will not be able to translate the word "spirit" when it is meant to signify both the "soul" and the liquid you put in your glass on a Friday night for example! So we might not be able to use computer-assisted translation programmes for our type of translation, but there is no doubt that the use of a computer is essential. I don't think there are any translators left who do it by hand, not even any left who use a typewriter with all the associated problems of carbon copies/photocopies and the notorious "Tipp-ex". Word processing packages are extremely helpful, as I said earlier, for writing in columns for example and help when you need to assess the length of your translation in the absence of time codes. The word count function is also essential to count the words of the source material for billing purposes. On the matter of counting words, there is nothing more frustrating than being given an Excel file to translate. Excel was designed to crunch numbers by the same clever people who designed Word to deal with words. I find it hard to believe that so many companies produce word documents on Excel, but this is the reality of life. Translators have had to train themselves to use Excel, when really Word should have been enough. And to count words in Excel was very difficult and time consuming. I said was, because, I have just been informed that a company called Translation3000 has brought out AnyCount, a Project Management program which produces automatic word counts for many common files, including Excel. I have just tested it and I can confirm that it works even better than expected.

So IT creates problems and then solves them a couple of years later! The spellchecker is another example of a good tool we can all use. They now come on CDs and you can have almost all languages on one CD at a very reasonable price. (However, you need to buy a new Proofing Tool CD every time you change your operating software. No comment!) Beware, they are very good tools but they have their limits. As a Frenchman with the tendency to drop my "h" or put them where they are not, I can easily be lulled into a false sense of security. For example if I write "ear" instead of "hear" or "arm" instead of "harm" the computer is very unlikely to help me as these words all exist in English. Also make sure the spellchecker is switched on to the right English – UK English or US English. In my computer I have a choice of eighteen different types of English. The same applies to Spanish (twenty different options) or French and many other languages which have differences depending on the regions involved. IT does help us tremendously for our writing. I remember having a hard time when I set myself the task of translating a book as an exercise. I met Margaret Drabble when she needed to go to Belgium and wanted to refresh her spoken French and she heard there was a young Frenchman around, so she asked me to help her with her conversational French. It ensued that I started to read all her books and during my next holiday, I decided to translate *The Garrick Year*. I suppose the reason I liked that novel so much is that it is set in the acting profession on the one hand and that on the other it touches very much on the issue of women's liberation in the '60s. To come back to the point, I did this translation using a cheap portable typewriter and it was…terrible! I had never had any practice at typing at the time and I learnt the hard way, using bottles of Tipp-ex in the process. As to the quality of the translation, absolutely awful! I fell for all the pitfalls of the untrained translator, but I nevertheless enjoyed it very much and learnt a lot on the way. A word processing package then would have been incredibly helpful and would have helped me produce a better translation. Humans being what they are, if it is easy to make a small correction then one makes it, if it is difficult, one tries to get away with it!!! I was no different. I am convinced that youngsters starting now have a better chance to provide better copy, because they can concentrate one hundred per cent on the quality of the work as they don't have to contend with the almost impossible task of correcting a typewritten document.

When I first started writing professionally, I used to make a handwritten copy and then type it, but it took such a long time! So however much I like the past, I love using computers! Even with the advent of computers in the early '80s (I got my first one in 1981) many of my colleagues carried on doing their translations by hand before entering them in the computer, I don't think there are any left who do that now. At first, I rented a dedicated word processor for about three months. I was a little bit worried about buying it; it was very expensive and the printer, a dot-matrix, was part of the machine. I thought the circuit boards would break because of the shaking produced by this type of printer. I made some enquiries and realised that for about the same amount of money, maybe a little bit more, I could buy a fully-fledged computer which would ultimately allow me to do much more that just typing. So after the trial period I acquired my first computer.

The software I acquired was difficult to use; it was called Samna III. The reason I chose it was that it was the only one that could electronically convert my keyboard to an azerty keyboard giving me the accents at one single touch instead of having to enter them by pressing ASCII codes on the numerical pad. I am sure many of you reading this now have never heard of ASCII, or DOS, but in those days you had to know about these things to make your computer work. There were not as many shortcuts as now; instead there were a lot of codes and commands to enter manually. The word Icon only meant the sacred portraits seen in the Eastern

Churches! Samna III became Samna IV and by the end of the
'80s this software started to have capabilities that were only achieved
by Microsoft many years later. I finally gave up on Samna when
it was gobbled up by another huge manufacturer. I knew that
programme so well, that it was not unusual for people to call me
to help them to sort out their problems with it. I was also quite
lucky that Samna had offices a mile away from me in Perivale.
This was really helpful when it broke down one day and I went
to their offices with my five-inch floppy disk and was able to have
them print the script I had to send away the same evening.

The Internet was not there yet, not quite, and we still had very
human relations with large manufacturing companies like Samna.
I say the Internet was not quite there, but at the time two Canadians,
the twin brothers Rook, put together a network of translators and
companies wanting to exchange documents using telephone lines.
I was one of the first to join, my address i.d. was something like
TXT097. We then started to exchange translations with colleagues
and clients. It was not very easy, we all had to acquire modems,
but they were all different and many settings had to be configured
manually to make sure they would talk to each other. Some
colleagues, including Werner Volkmer, used a telephone coupler
to link their computer to the handset of their telephone. I must
admit that in these early days the time we gained in not using
the Royal Mail was spent trying to make the communication system
work, but in the end we managed to exchange our documents
quite successfully.

But for people using foreign languages with accents, there was
a big problem: the accents were not carried through the system;
they were not recognised because they were using the eighth bit
of information. You remember when I mentioned ASCII, well ASCII
characters use seven bits of information and the eighth one is used
to check technically that the transmission has worked. That could
not work with the accented letters which were also using the eighth
bit. A solution had to be found and someone did. One of our
colleagues developed a programme whereby each of the accented
characters would be encoded into a couple of ASCII recognisable

characters. For example you would have é equal e{. You only needed to have the same programme doing the decoding the other end and your file would be readable. When the Internet came on the market and started to be used by the public at large this was still very much an issue, which is why so many people have got used to writing their e-mails without any accents. There is a certain amount of laziness attached to that now, but originally it was impossible to do it as your message would not have gone through. It took years before you could send a translation as an attachment with all your accents and be assured that it would arrive in a readable format at its destination.

Some of you might remember that for many years most translators were using CompuServe to send their translation. Well the reason they were not eager to change, even when it did not work very well, was that all CompuServe users could exchange their translations without any problems. If you had to send your accented script to someone using another account it did not work and that went on well into the mid-'90s. I had once to translate into FIGS (that is an acronym meaning French Italian German Spanish). This acronym is used because these four languages are the main ones we work in when doing corporate productions. In our terms this work was big: 20,000 words to translate into the four languages. The client called me months ahead of the production and asked me not only for the cost but also how long it would take to do the job. So I told him that on average a translator would do two thousand words a day and that we therefore needed forty days. I also insisted that we would need to have CompuServe addresses in each of the countries concerned to be able to deliver the translations. He said that would not be a problem.

A few months later he called back and told us we had the contract and that the translations were needed three weeks later. Well that was not unusual, but this time there was also Easter bang in the middle of the three weeks! I contacted the translators and we worked hard to meet the deadline. The Spanish was the first to be ready so I asked for the CompuServe address to be forwarded to me. I received an e-mail back telling me that the Internet address was so and so. I replied that it would not work. I tried to send the translation to Spain and it did not work. I therefore asked the Spanish recipient to send me a CompuServe address and a few minutes later they had the script and could revise the translation. Then the French was ready on a Friday at eleven in the morning. No CompuServe address was available. The French editor called me on the phone and was adamant that there should not be any problem sending the translation to the e-mail address he had given me. I told him I was in front of my computer and he only needed to tell me what to do. We worked until seven-thirty trying to send the translation, at which point he finally said he had a friend who had a CompuServe account on the other side of Paris, he gave me the address and the translation was in Paris within minutes. Now wait for it... the client in Paris was a major international computer manufacturer!

Once the big service providers sorted the problem out, translators started to use many different Internet Service Providers and could change them as often as they liked knowing that there would not be any basic problem in communicating with their clients. Computers do help us, they speed our work up and allow us to work better and on the whole they are now pretty reliable, but you still need to make back-up copies of everything you do. If you have worked hard on a translation, you must make a copy in the evening. I now have an external back-up which runs automatically every night, so in case of a breakdown of the hard disk, only a minimal amount of work would be lost, if anything at all. IT has revolutionised the World, and it has not passed us by. I find writing and translating using a computer is much more fun than when I had to do the translations by hand and then type them.

To transcribe

In relation to typing you might be required to do some transcriptions. From time to time a client will come up with an interview made in a foreign language and will want to know the content. In the past, the client would have sent you (and that still happens today, but less and less) a VHS. It is a little bit difficult to handle as you need a TV and a video player close to your computer. On a VHS machine it is difficult to go back with precision and a lot of time is wasted on fiddling with the equipment. A good machine to do transcription would have been a Betacam, but we are here talking about professional video equipment used in editing suites and that was not affordable to translators. Translators only tend to use this equipment if clients ask them to come and do the job on location in their offices. So when asked to transcribe a VHS I have always asked the client to send me an audio cassette as well, as it is much easier to handle, but it was not always possible for the client to do that. If that was the case I wired my TV set very simply, using one of the output channels to plug into a cassette recorder and made my own audio copy.

It was time well spent as transcribing from the audio is so much faster than doing it from the VHS. I only used the video when I could not quite understand what the speaker was saying, hoping to be able to lip-read the offending part. You could play the audio on a normal cassette player or on a Dictaphone type of machine, which made the transcription much easier. However, a good Dictaphone can be pretty expensive. I used a simple foot pedal connected to my Sony Walkman Professional for years. It was good enough to make broadcast quality interviews, which in my case was the primary use, and also very good as a dictating machine. Nowadays all this has become obsolete. All can be done on the computer. Instead of receiving a VHS or an audio tape you are more likely to receive an .mp3, a .wma or a .wav file.[2] You will be able to play these on your computer; the problem is that you will not be able to type the script into your Word document at the same time.

However, there are ways around that. In the old days (I now mean six months ago: the perception of time is changing very rapidly in our modern technological age) I used one computer to play the sound and another one to write the script. It was a bit fiddly and not all together satisfactory. Remember that as a translator that sort of thing is not going to happen very often and that you do this job only as a favour to a good client, or to attract a new one. However, if you feel the demand is there and you might have a few more translations if you can offer this service then it might become much more practical and make economic sense to invest in a dedicated software program and a pedal to tackle this task.

I am using something called DSS Player Pro Transcription Module from the Olympus Corporation. It is a wonderful tool as you can use one computer to do both operations. It costs about two hundred pounds that you will rapidly recoup as you will be able to transcribe much faster and start making your money on translating the transcription. Here again I suggest you create a document with two or three columns. In the first one, write the transcription, in the second one your translation and in the third one your comments. Once the transcription is finished, you need to put the time code at the beginning of each paragraph or sentence, as this will help your client know **what** the interviewee is saying **when**.

You will also have to establish with your client what the end use of the translation is. He might want to make subtitles or a voice-over. As a foreign translator you will be confronted with a little problem here. Can you actually translate into English as an English person born and bred? You need to decide with your client how you are going to tackle this problem. You can tell them, "Look I can transcribe the script for you, I can make a translation that will tell you exactly what the interviewee is saying, but I am not a native writer of English and you might want to tweak the script to make it perfect."

In my experience clients are very often satisfied by this approach. They only want to know what the guy is saying and when. They very often know what they want the interviewee to say, so it is only a question of finding the right place and then they will deal with the English. The other option is to offer the full service to your client without bothering them with that and working with an English translator who is going to revise your copy. You also need to establish if your client wants everything that has been recorded: the false starts, the sentences that don't get anywhere, the hums and the hesitations and so on. In many cases they will ask you to transcribe only the parts that are usable and here you might need after all to have a look at the video as a beautiful sounding sentence might not be usable because the camera fell at that stage, the light was switched off or the mic came into the field of vision and so on. So back to the VHS!

Well, no, I just had a case where I could not quite make out a word; it turned out to be an abbreviation I had not encountered before. I told the client that the sound of the file they had sent me was a little bit compressed and that maybe they could just send me that sentence as a high quality uncompressed file, but he gave me instead a link to the video which was on the Internet. I was able to watch the interview and as it very often happens, I could make out the word by looking at the speaker's lips.

In the studio

Technology helps ever more in the studio as well. When recording the soundtrack on a Sadie for example, nothing is normally lost. A Sadie is one of the professional computers used to record sound in studios. From time to time something might get lost, but it is very rare, so when you do a retake, you can still revert to the old take if necessary. With this type of recording system you can drop in and even edit "on the fly". Edit on the fly, means that the SM can for example reposition the recording while you are still recording. As mentioned earlier, when you take a cue, whether audio or a cue light, there is a little delay, and the SM is able to move the voice back to where it should have started even before you have finished that take. I should say **some** SMs are able to do that. You need a lot of experience and confidence in your equipment to do it, but I work with many sound engineers who are able to do that. IT is also extremely useful for recording phrase synch and even more for lip-synch. It can help match the lip movement by expanding or contracting the recording without changing the pitch of the voice. In the old days that was not possible:

if you merely accelerated or slowed the recording, it affected the voice. You probably have heard what happened when the battery goes flat on a portable Discman or cassette player. That of course was not very useful. The editing is so sophisticated nowadays that little noises can be cut out manually or through the usage of gates. Gates are filters which will take out certain types of noises or frequencies that were recorded by mistake on the hard disk. There are many other functions that help the sound engineer produce a clean recording and ultimately make the work of the voice easier. In the past, it would have been necessary to retake some sentences or paragraphs that can now be cleaned by the SM, so it is more work for him and less for you! It also means that we can record longer scripts than before within a one-hour session, thus bringing the production costs down a bit. In the long run it means that we record more for the same amount of money, but that is the way things are going in this industry as in many others.

Building your own studio

Now if like most translators you are not frightened of computers, you could contemplate using them to install your own studio. However, before you actually build your own studio, you could start at a lower entry level. You could buy some editing software. This has two advantages: you would be able to learn to edit, and once you have built up your confidence in that department you could start recording yourself in your own office. The second advantage is that you would spend less time in the studio you rent for the actual recording session. The studio would give you your recording on a CD or you could even bring your own CD to keep the cost down. Once home you could then spend time editing on your own equipment. To build your own studio there are two levels; the first one is to create your own recording studio. We had them at the BBC and they were called "self ops", in other words they are studios that you can operate yourself to record your own voice! The other level is to build an ISDN booth so that studios around the world can connect to your system and record you. And all this in the comfort of your own environment! Having said all that, it might in fact be easier to start with an ISDN booth. The reason being that once installed (you could have it done by a professional), you would not have to worry about editing, just switching on and waiting for your client to dial in and start speaking your script into the microphone. Nevertheless, if you decide to start by becoming your own studio engineer, I would suggest you begin with a pretty good computer running on Windows XP with a large hard disk, or preferably two, so that you do not run out of memory. Quality sound files do take a lot of space on your computer, especially if you compare them to Word files. The other option is to have a computer entirely dedicated to your recordings, but that I think will come when you start doing a lot of voices at home. In either case, it is very important to install a good quality sound card in your computer. This may provide some sort of internal "mini mixer", or perhaps additional cables for plugging a good quality microphone or mixer straight in. There are also now many high-quality USB interfaces available at reasonable cost which plug directly into your computer with a USB plug and into which you can then plug your microphone.

It will be easier for you to become a "studio engineer" if you have been working in many studios and had a good look at what is going on. I am not talking here about buying a Sadie. This is the maker of dedicated sound recording computers which used to be very expensive. Prices have gone down and of course there could always be a second-hand one on the market. However, I think you would need serious training in studio engineering to work with a professional computer like this one. No, I want to share with you my experience of using a normal PC. In fact I am using one which is not very recent and which runs on Windows 98 for recording purposes.

When you start training you can use the existing sound card and the jacks that are provided with most computers nowadays (see opposite page) . You can easily recognise them in the picture as I have left fingers in the frame to give you a good idea of the size of the jack I am talking about. Nonetheless, I think you will need to invest in some software and hardware to obtain a good quality recording as soon as you intend to deliver professional recordings acceptable to your clients.

As software I am using Cool Edit Pro. Cool Edit has been taken over by Adobe and is called Adobe Audition but is still very similar. I have downloaded the trial version of Audition and I don't think you will find anything very different in it. There seems to be an additional option to make CDs that was not included in Cool Edit and also some more tools in the *Studio,* but that's about all. I am not going to tell you about the *Studio* as you don't really need to know about it at this stage. It is a Multitrack viewer which allows you to mix your voice with music or sound effects, which is not something clients are going to ask you to do, unless you decide to change profession all together and become a sound mixer, in which case you need to go back to school and start studying the subject from scratch. There are many other programmes on the market, some may perform better, but are also more difficult to use and also more expensive. Cool Edit Pro is easy to use to do the basic recording and editing of a voice recording, and later you will also be able to add a music and effect track if you so wish. Cool Edit Pro could be downloaded from the Internet or bought in a shop. You can now do the same for Adobe Audition.

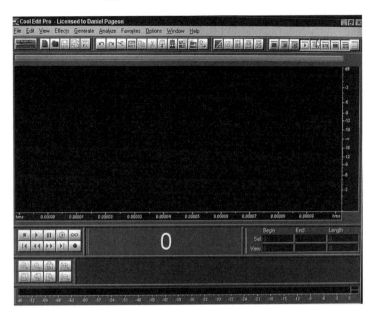

Let's have a look at the opening screen of Cool Edit Pro.

Cool Edit is quite intuitive and the thinking behind it is not dissimilar to using a Microsoft program. I am going to talk you through doing your first recording.

You will have to click on the Icon of a "page" which is yellow on my version of Cool Edit; it is the second button from the left under the word "View". It will create a blank wave file with a window in the middle of the screen where you will have to select three options.

I normally select a Sample Rate of 44100 KHz (as used on CDs), then the Mono Channel (as we have only one voice) and then a 16 bit resolution and I click on OK. Most clients will be happy with these specifications. You will very rarely be asked to change them, but in case a client needs something different you will only need to click on the relevant information. They might ask you for a higher sample rates, or for a lower one, or to have the file in stereo. You only need to click in front of the specification to get the little black spot and the specifications will have been changed accordingly. These changes will affect the size of the file, but this is not a problem for you.

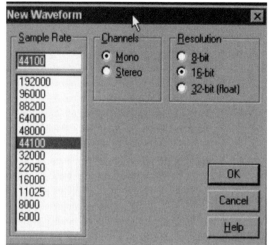

After that you will find, situated at the bottom left of your screen, a number of buttons which look the same as on any recorders with the usual buttons for play, fast forward and rewind and of course the round Red Button for record, this is the last one on the right on the bottom line.

Click on the round Red Button and start recording.

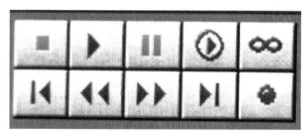

Once you have done your recording you will need to save it. I suggest you save all your sessions before you start editing. To save you go to *File*, and click on *Save Copy as* ....

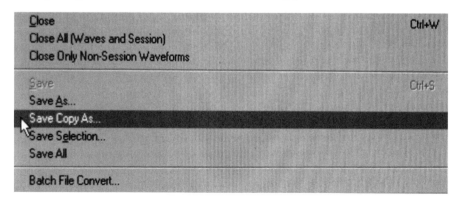

In *Save in* you will select the folder into which you wish to save your file. As is the case with Word documents, when you work on your translations, I highly recommend you use a classification system that will allow you to keep your files and find them again a few years later if you have to. Everyone will have slightly different preferences. It does not really matter how you organise your files, as long as you do file them and you can find them again!

... a new window will open.

Then you enter the name of your file in *File name* (try to use names that are useful and easily recognisable) and you can add the language into which you have been recording as well before sending the file to a client. Remember that you can use more than eight characters to name your files, so the title can be very descriptive.

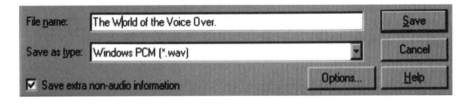

You will then need to fill in the *Save as type* window. It is here that the wave files I have been talking so much about appear. You will select *Windows PCM (*.wav)* in the dropdown menu, for your own work. It might be, of course, that a client asks you for another of the files listed in the menu. I suggest you then save it in the required format. You should not have to touch the *Options* button when you save in *Windows PCM (*.wav)*. You then only need to click on *Save* and bingo! You have your recording.

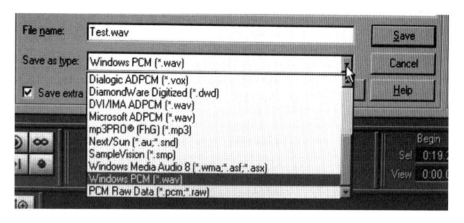

If you are a bit paranoid like me, you will probably make a copy of the recording straight away in another area of your hard disk, or on another computer if you have a second one, or on a memory stick if the file is small enough or the stick large enough, or you could "burn" the recording into a CD or a DVD. This ensures that you can edit to your heart's content and if you do erase something accidentally, you can always recover it from your safety copy. There is an undo function on Cool Edit, so you can always go back if you have made minor mistakes. I am talking here about deleting a file or getting mixed up with names. To make CDs or DVDs you need to have the relevant writers. CD and DVD drives are now cheap and so are the writers. You will be able to make CDs on a DVD writer as well as DVDs and they come with their own software so that should not be a problem.

I remember once working on a long recording with a Farsi speaker. We had two files to record; one was quite short and the other one very long with a similar name. It was late and I got distracted and saved the short file which was finished under the name of the long file, so losing the entire content of the long file, three hours worth of recording. Well, luckily we did not have to go through the session again, because I was running a DAT tape recorder as well and recorded the entire session as a safety copy! I was therefore able to recover the deleted material. However, I had to spend quite a bit of time editing the file anew as there were a lot of takes. The advantage of this was that I did not need to recall the voice for a full recording session, which would have cost me the earth. I only booked her for a very short time to check that I had edited the files correctly. I suggest you add a DAT (Digital Audio Tape) to your system if you start using other people to come in to record as you would have to pay them their session fee again if you lost their recording for any reason and that is costly. If you are the only one doing the recordings, then it will mean revoicing the parts of files you have lost. It will cost you a bit of time, but you will not have to fork out a lot of cash. A DAT deck is quite expensive and you need to connect it to your system. It is not terribly difficult to do, but it takes yet a little bit more room, and generally speaking translators do not have huge offices at home. Furthermore, DAT tapes are very expensive. They were used a lot for a short period before CD and DVD recorders became affordable and easy to use. I don't think many people use DAT any more except for the backing up application I have been talking about. Another option these days, is to use a dedicated audio CD burner as a secondary backup whilst recording, but I have not yet tried it myself.

So, once you have your backup copy, you can start to edit your recording. You will want to delete the takes that were no good and also double-check that there aren't any noises you did not want, like clicks and other sounds a reader might make unwittingly. If they are between words, they can be easily cut out or replaced by a bit of the wave that only contains atmos (that is short for atmosphere) in other words the sound emitted by your studio when no one is speaking. If you cut a bit of the sound wave, your words might come too close to each other and the cut might be heard, so replacing the unwanted noise by a bit of atmos is a good option. Cool Edit also has the facility to "Silence" a section of the recording. If the noise is right in the middle of the word, in other words under your voice, it is going to be fiddly to remove, it might even be impossible, in which case you will need to do a retake. When you are recording yourself you should wear a pair of cans (headphones) and listen carefully for any extraneous noises to avoid having to redo bits of your recording afterwards, which is always a bit frustrating. To actually delete a part of the wave, you only need to highlight it. I can hear you screaming at me: "What does he mean highlight it?" I know because that sort of explanation made me very upset and still makes me very upset! Manuals tell you to do something, thinking you automatically know what they mean! I will try not to fall into that category, but I must admit it is easy to stumble into that trap. So to highlight a section of the wave, you position the cursor at the beginning of the part you wish to delete, you then press on the left-hand-side button on your mouse and you drag the cursor, keeping the button pressed, to the end of the part you want to delete and then you click on the delete button on your keyboard. (By the way there is a safety net I have alluded to earlier on: it is the redo function and is represented by the same curved arrow you find in MSWord. It is very useful because sometimes when you play back after you have deleted a bit you discover that you do not like what you hear and you want to start again. Do watch out though for a very similar looking button with a back arrow and a "no-entry" sign. If this is not pressed in, you will not have the redo function available.)

Now, I have told you that deleting a bit of the wave might distort the delivery as it will bring the words closer together; so to avoid that you need to *copy and paste*.

	Begin	End	Length
Sel	0:00.000	0:11.520	0:11.520
View	0:00.000	0:11.520	0:11.520

First you need to look at the length of the segment you wish to replace. To do that you highlight the portion you want to replace and you look into the windows at the bottom right hand side of the Cool Edit screen. There are six boxes; the length of the highlighted section will appear directly under the word *length*. You make a mental note of this length (or you write it down) and you find a bit of the wave where there is nothing recorded and you then copy it. To copy a bit of wave of the same length you highlight the part of the wave you need until you obtain the same figure in the length box. You then click on the left button of the mouse and click on *Copy*. You then move to the portion you want to replace, you highlight it again to the same length and you then *Paste*. After a bit of practice this can be done very quickly and of course the better your original recording the faster the editing will be.

By the way, I think I mentioned before that I took to using the mouse quite late, but I use it all the time now. However, for people who like to use shortcuts on the keyboard, there are two I find very useful: the *Copy* and the *Paste* one. To *Copy* you simply need to hold down *Control* and then press *C* and for *Paste* you hold down *Control* and press *V*. (If you used *Control* and *P*, you would print a document!) Another point I would like to mention to make your editing easier is that you can actually change the shape of the wave by making it longer, so that the space to cut out, which might have been tiny, will look quite large.

To expand the wave on-screen you only need to use some of the buttons at the bottom left of the screen. There are eight of them. The first one on the top row has a + sign in the middle. If you click on it the wave will become larger (you can click more than once), and you will be able to see its content in more detail. The − button will reduce the wave and the third button with nothing in the middle will make the entire wave fit into the computer window. (An alternative if you have a wheel on the top of your mouse is to roll the wheel away from you to expand the waveform.) The two buttons with the vertical arrows enlarge the wave horizontally. You need to make the wave large enough so that you can see clearly that the voice is not peaking, i.e. being recorded too loud, which would distort the sound. That would translate visually as well; you would see the wave going over the two horizontal lines, either at the bottom or at the top of the screen or both. The wave should remain within the two horizontal white lines on your screen. You can also make sure that the recording is being done at the right level by looking at the bottom right hand side of your screen.

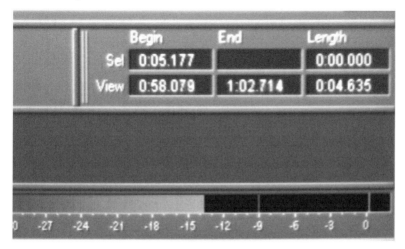

The green line keeps moving horizontally when sound is being recorded, from left to right. The green becomes red when it hits 0. You should test the recording and try to keep the maximum between about -6 and -3. However, as long as the line does not turn red and does not hit the 0 decibel you are all right. On the picture this is the grey line at the bottom which peaks between -15 and - 12.

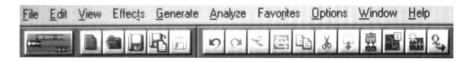

To check that your recording is within the accepted sound quality parameters in the industry you can click on *Analyse*, but before doing that you must highlight the entire file. This can be done by double clicking on the left button of your mouse. The highlighted part will then be analysed. In the picture on the right you can see the resulting statistics.

Do not be frightened by the number of figures and boxes you have to look at. The first one to read is the third box from the top *Peak Amplitude* with the figure - 1.83 dB. This is the one which should not reach zero. The next one is called *Possible Clipped*

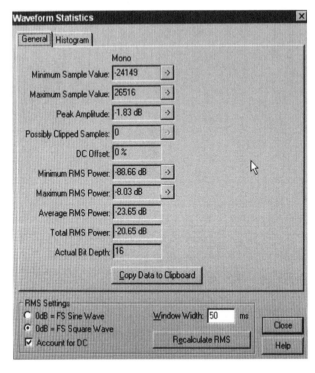

Samples with the figure zero. It is the right result. If you had one or more clipped samples that would mean some of the words might be distorted and that is not acceptable at a professional level. The next box to look at is *Minimum RMS Power*; the result here is - 88.66 dB. This result is within the acceptable range. This is really a measure of how much total noise you have on your recordings. You may hear the term "signal to noise ratio" (SNR). This is in fact the ratio between your voice and the noise, or on these statistics, the Minimum and Maximum RMS Power. They use a negative scale called dB, where 0 is maximum volume, and −20dB is louder than −40dB. The larger the Minimum Power number going towards −100 or more is, the better the recording. If you had a reading of −70dB or less (closer to 0) you might have your recording rejected by your client. This in effect measures the total noise coming from your studio system. It is not a noise you are going to hear on the small loudspeakers you are using with your computer, but if your client was going to broadcast your recording on very large speakers in a conference hall for example it would be heard. Having said that, a client with that sort of project would most probably go to a fully professional studio. Nevertheless, I don't think you should send recordings with noise levels between -70dB and 0. You might be recording with the Minimum RMS Power (noise) at say -55 and not even realize that there is a noise. So check your system to make sure you obtain good results. I will mention hardware to improve on these results a little bit later.

You may also be asked by clients to provide them with an MP3 file. An MP3 (or MPEG) file is a sound file that has been compressed so that you can send it by e-mail. Files which are over five megabytes in size might not get out of your own system or might be rejected by the ISP (Internet Service Provider) if you try to email them. For technical reasons, files which leave your computer become even larger when they are sent via the Internet. You therefore need to compress them, but of course you want to lose as little as possible of the quality you have worked so hard to achieve. MP3 is one of the solutions which can be implemented easily with Cool Edit. You will open your wave file and then save it as an MP3 file. On the version of Cool Edit Pro I use, there are some options you will need to choose. But first you open the dropdown menu in *Save as type* and you select mp3PRO(FhG). You will then need to click on *Options* and select the one you want. The best one, which will be almost as good as a wave file, is *128Kbps, 44100 Hz, Mono*. You will see in between brackets (5.5:1): this indicates the compression ratio, in other words the file will be 5.5 times smaller than the original wav. If it is for demonstration purposes only you might want to compress more. When you restart Cool Edit, it will have kept the previous settings, so if you have done a recording as indicated before and if you go into *Save as* and select MP3, you will not have to change the *Options*. It will be set as the last options you had selected. You are now ready to send your recording to your client; you can send it as an attachment to your e-mail, just like a Word file or any other documents. However, if the file is still bigger than five meg, it might not be possible to send it by e-mail at all. There are a number of options to send the file to the client. The one I use quite successfully at the moment is FTP, File Transfer Protocol.

There are other transmission methods coming up, but I have not used them yet. The advantage of working with FTP is that most clients will have one set up and they will send a link for you to follow to upload your file. You can also quite easily set up your own FTP server on your computer. The software is available for free and you can download it from the Internet. This is useful when your client does not have an FTP server running. You are then the one sending the link to the client. The client will then download the file from your FTP site, which can be based on your own computer or on a remote site on the Internet. Your ISP will probably provide you with some free space to house your FTP site, but if not, it is just as easy to have the FTP on your own computer. Once your client has downloaded the file, you close your FTP. You must be aware that the client is going to come into your computer; some people do not like that idea. The way to protect yourself is to only give access to the folder where you have deposited the file you want your client to access. The client will need a password to download it. To go anywhere else would require the skills of a hacker! For peace of mind, you will find that it is easy to know when your client has downloaded the file and once that has been done successfully you just close the door by switching off the FTP and you are safe again. The other option is, of course, to make a CD or a DVD of the file and send it courtesy of the Royal Mail or other messenger services. CD and DVD writers are now quite cheap and so are the actual discs, in fact the postage is going to cost you more than the discs themselves! But that also means it is going to take more time to be delivered, especially if your client is based on the other side of the planet.

BUT, before you can actually record you will have to plug in a microphone. Computers very often come with a small one but they tend not to be good enough to give you a professional sound. Nonetheless, for the sake of training and in order not to have to spend all your money in one go, you can start with that little one. Remember that the quality of the microphone is extremely important to the quality of the end product. There are a number of factors that will dictate the choice of microphone you will buy. I think the first one is the acoustics of the room you are using. To improve the acoustics of your cubicle you will have to make sure that as little noise from outside comes into it. To achieve that perfectly you would need to build an anechoic room. This is a room which is suspended in the air! As noise travels through solid materials, if you could put a room without any physical contact with the outside walls, and a vacuum in between it would be perfect. That cannot be done, so you will try to have as few contacts with the ground and with the other walls as possible. As you can imagine, this is very rarely possible at home, as you would need quite a large space to build it.

To be more realistic, you are more likely to build a cubicle under your staircase or in a corner of your study. If you can add two walls in a corner of a room, that would be a good start. A way to deaden the sound and stop a lot of outside noise is to line your walls (including the ceiling and floors) with a very heavy material called Acoustilay. It comes in different depths. I have used the 15mm one and it did cut out a lot of the noise. I have also glued some panels of it on the doors to stop even more noise coming into the cubicle. But that is not all; you should also make sure the inside walls are not reflecting the noise too much; you might have some parts of walls that are flat, but try to have some absorbent material on some other parts, like old curtains with nice folds (all this will add to a comfy atmosphere to the studio). There are of course very expensive professional absorbing materials that could be used, but you can probably get away with the old curtains. These days, you can get professional acoustic tiles of various qualities at reasonable prices from companies like Studio Spares, and you don't need many to cover a small cubicle. Another good way to make sure the sound does not reverberate around the room is to use some square egg cartons; you can obtain them free when you buy your eggs! It is also a good idea to have a table covered with some sound-absorbing material rather than a flat desk. You can buy some custom made, but you could make yourself one very easily by covering a table with a blanket. It is important that the table should not creak; the same also applies to the chair. It is important to have a carpet on the floor rather than tiles or wood.

Another little thing you need to take care of is the relative position of the light to the script. You will want to have as much light as possible on your script, but the lamp must be positioned in such a way that you do not have the shadow of the microphone, or anything else for that matter, projected on your piece of paper. I suppose I am becoming more and more sensitive to this with the passing of the years! This seems quite obvious, but you would be surprised at how many superb studios, with the latest equipment available on the market, have forgotten about that little thing. They have only thought in terms of hardware and software and forgotten that a human being is going to sit behind the mic and will have to read the script.

If you have built yourself a soundproof room, you will want a microphone that will pick up the atmosphere as well as your voice and give you a warm sound. The first microphone I bought was a Rode NT2. It is an excellent microphone, made in Australia, which gives value for money. As I wanted to have a back-up mic, in case my first one needed to be serviced or broke down, I bought an AGK C 414. This one was more expensive as it is made in Germany, but I liked it so much that since I actually plugged it in to test it I have only changed it once so far for a specific client who preferred the sound of the Rode NT2 for a recording down the line (that is another way of saying you are using the ISDN lines).

For real emergencies, in cases where I had to do recordings with a lot of noise around, like jumbo jets flying overhead, I tried a Shure SM7A. It is almost like a lip mic, the type used by horse racing or other sporting commentators who work in very noisy environment. This type of microphone might be just about all right if your recording is going to have a loud music and effects track but it is not going to work if it is for audio only. I have been asked to work with a lip microphone a few times when the client did not have a sound recording studio and asked the voice to come to the editing suite. As you can imagine it is quite disorientating to be working in a noisy environment when people are doing other things in the same room. The sound is not great, but because there is so much happening on the tape already, it seems to work…more or less!!! Remember that the microphone is the first part in the recording sequence. If it is poor quality, all your recordings will be poor quality, whatever expensive equipment or sound-proofing you use for the rest of your studio. It should probably be one of the most expensive items you buy.

If you are using your office which you think is quiet, there are no noises coming from outside and nothing is making too much noise in the room itself, then you might want to go for a unidirectional microphone into which you'll speak from quite close. Once you start listening you will be surprised by the amount of noise there is in a quiet room. I remember doing a series of interviews in Canada in the early '80s. Some of them were in public places or outside and that was fine but one of them was on the thirty-second floor of a large corporation in a very quiet room and of course I could pick up the sound of the air conditioning. When I asked the managing director if it was at all possible to get rid of this very loud noise, he said he had never noticed it until I pointed it out, and of course he could not stop the system in his room, it would have to be in the entire building and that was not possible, obviously! This is just to say that when you start listening for something, you will no doubt hear it. I cannot say that my hearing has improved with the passing of years, but I certainly can say that my awareness of surrounding noises has improved dramatically.

Remember that any recording in an office environment, or close to your recording computer, is going to have the noise of the computer on it. Just stop for a moment now, and listen to the noise the fans make on your computer.

To achieve a good sound, and to be able to control the type of sound you produce, you will also need to acquire a sound equaliser. I went for the Focusrite VoiceMaster because it combines a mic preamplifier (shortened to preamp), a dynamics unit and an equaliser. You will need quite a bit of time and effort to set all the different knobs to the right levels. You will of course have a user's guide with the equipment and you will have to trust your ears. You might also want to do a few tests with people who are used to listening to sound files. They will tell you if they hear something they don't like. Of course you might have conflicting reports, so you will need to make up your own mind and take notes, as some clients might prefer more of this or more of that. However, once you are happy with the way your voice sounds, you should not have to change the settings much. It becomes much more complicated if you need to record different people, because male and female sound different for a start, and then people project more or less. As the sole user of your equipment you should be able to sort things out to run very smoothly. Little things like how far you sit from the microphone, and at which angle you are going to poise it will become obvious and you will not have to keep changing these things.

As a rule of thumb, the less hardware you put between the microphone and the computer the better the sound should be for your home recording.

However, you will very soon want to improve the sound quality of your system and you might want to acquire some better hardware. I think it would be a good idea to buy a professional sound card [or USB interface] for the computer as it will produce a sound quality that will be acceptable for many applications. You might

also want to use XLR connectors rather than small pins or jacks.

An XLR is quite a large connector, it is sturdy and will not move out very easily as there is a locking mechanism between the male and the female ends; the wiring will be stronger and is going to last for a long time. It is also essential if you need to run the microphone or recording signal over any distance, as it is far less affected by electrical noise than the home audio jacks.

Your cables should be of good quality. They should be long enough so that you do not have to pull on them, but the shorter they are the better, as you will lose quality over a long stretch of cable. Not a lot, but it all adds up to getting you closer to this dreaded − 70dB noise level! Remember: your aim is to get as far as possible from it, − 75dB or − 80dB being good.

Another little piece of equipment you might want to install before going for the ISDN connection is a "coupler". This is known as a "patch box" also "telephone hybrid" or Telephone Balance Unit (TBU) to connect a normal telephone line into your system. It is quite easy to install a coupler; and, what's more, it is a small box so you do not have to worry too much about the space it is going to take. It will not be connected between your mic and your recording system, so the quality of the recording will not be affected at all by this addition. With this system your clients can be listening to your recording on the phone and direct you. The director will not have any control over the technical quality of the recording, but he will be able to direct your performance, which might be extremely useful if the client is very specific about the type of delivery required or if you do not have a lot of experience at directing yourself.

Once you are happy with your studio and the recordings go well, you might want to give studios around the world the opportunity to work with you by installing an ISDN link. To do that you will need to rent the ISDN lines and buy a Codec − this stands for coder/decoder. The Coder encodes the analogue voice signal into a digital signal, and the Decoder does the same thing in reverse at the other end, to allow your clients to record your voice on their own computer. Working this way you can do "wild" recordings (recordings are called "wild" when we do not record to pictures or to time codes) or you can listen in to a guide track and follow it, just like in a traditional studio where you record to pictures. Sometimes clients are concerned that you do not see the video while you are recording. You can reassure them by explaining that even when you have access to the video, you do not really have the time to watch the film as you are looking at your script, listening to the original track and producing the narration in your own language. There is really no time to watch the video!

There are many different types of Codec, and they have numerous settings to enable them to communicate between each other. Your choice will very much depend on the potential clients you have and on how much money you want to spend on the equipment. Once you think you are going to try to install your ISDN connection, do speak to your clients and ask them what they are using at their end to make up your mind. Having done my research in 1999, I decided to go for the Prima LT. It is compatible with almost everything else on the market and certainly was one of the few available then. This is not the type of equipment you are going to change very often; you want your investment to last a long time so that you can recover your cost quickly and start making money.

---

1   The book title in Italian is simply *Una Vita*.

2   They are all sound file formats which are more or less compressed [NB WAV is an uncompressed format, but the file size can be made smaller by varying the sample or bit rate], but tend to be good enough for the purpose of transcribing. Indeed the .wav format is top of the range, it is the format used to record the original. A wave file would need to be sent by FTP unless it was a very short interview; the quality of the original requires much more space than the compressed formats.

MARKETING
YOUR SERVICES

You probably already have some means of marketing your translation services and I suggest you carry on doing that if you are satisfied with the amount of work you are receiving that way. In terms of marketing your voice and your studio, there are a number of tools you might want to develop. But first I would suggest that before building your own studio, you might want to have a trial period. To do that you will need to find out if there is a studio reasonably close to your usual place of work. You should approach them and find out if they would be prepared to work with you; there is no reason why they should refuse, as you are a potential client. I suggest you start talking to them about what I call an "audio only" recording. This is what is requested by clients when no pictures are required and when there might not even be timing constraint. These are the simplest types of recordings. You would need to find out about the studio's costs. There are a number of costs involved. The recording cost is the first one, the editing cost is the second one and "stock" is the third one.

"Stock" is the generic word for any support material that is use to record the voice on. In the past I have used quarter-inch tape, then cassettes (which were not of a very high quality I must admit), and then we went on to DAT (Digital Audio Tape), and of course now CDs and lately DVDs. The ideal way (and cheapest!) for you would be to ask them to do the recording and transfer the data onto a CD that you could even bring along yourself. The word "data" is quite important here as you would find it difficult to transfer the content of an audio CD to your computer to edit it. Today blank CDs are very cheap, whereas a studio would charge you much more. The time of making the CD would also be added to the studio cost, but that will very much depend on the length of your recording. In any case, this will not make a huge difference to the total cost, but nothing must be forgotten in the very competitive global market we operate in. If you have already installed your recording software on your own computer, you should be able to edit your wave file and send the finished product to your client.

You would also need to know the cost of recording to vision; that is when you have to voice against pictures and make sure that everything fits perfectly. You might have to use the studio's services even when you are yourself fully operational with your audio studio. You will also need to find out if they have an ISDN connection, as this might be a necessary service to offer your clients around the world.

As a bonus, working with a local studio, you might just be lucky enough to have them ask you for help with their language requirements, as they might also have clients looking for foreign-language recordings. It is very much a two-way business and the snowball effect does work very well, it certainly has in my case. It is always a good idea to have a relationship with a local studio, even if you have set up your own studio and are totally confident you can do the recordings yourself. You might want to use them as a back-up. Equipment nowadays is very robust and reliable, but something might go wrong, and you would still need to deliver a recording very quickly, and might not have the time to sort out the problems before your delivery deadline. Therefore as a rule of thumb you should base your prices to your client around what it would cost you if you had to go to your local studio, this way if something goes wrong, you are not out of pocket and your client has not been affected. And you will not be undercutting the market either. (Offering your services for a cheaper price is in the long term a disaster in the making as there will always be someone doing it cheaper and you will find yourself working for nothing.

You should base your attractiveness on the quality of your service and not solely on the cut price you are offering.) You will be able to provide a seamless service even in case of a technical hitch.

Some of you might live in the country far from any studios. Well, nothing is perfect in life and you will have to cope with that and maybe travel a long way in an emergency. To reassure you, I have been operating my home studio for six years now, and touch wood, any little hiccoughs were resolved in time to deliver the files to the clients. So you should not be unduly concerned by the risk attached to breakdown of the hardware or the software.

In terms of marketing itself, I suggest you do the obvious, which is to tell your existing clients that you have a new service to offer. It is always a good idea to keep in touch with clients, especially the ones who don't contact you very often. It reminds them that you exist and offering a new service is a very impressive way to do it. You will be able to add to your services every now and again; first you will tell them you can offer them specialist translations for the spoken word. Then when you feel confident about your own voice you will inform them that you could do the voicing yourself and later on that you can even do some of the recordings in your own studio. Clients will probably be impressed by the way you are building up your knowledge and your skills. If they are satisfied with the results, they will no doubt mention it to other people in the industry and your name will start travelling around as someone who can take an original version and deliver it back not only on paper but on CD or whatever medium is requested. The entire operation being conducted under one roof makes life easier for clients who might not have much to input when dealing with a foreign version in a language they do not understand.

Looking for new clients has always been the biggest hurdle in any industry. However, I can give you a few pointers on the whereabouts of your potential clients. The agencies of course are the obvious one, but there are also other areas worth investigating. The first one might be the studios themselves. As I mentioned earlier, studios used to supply their clients with voices they knew because they had recorded in their studios before. Studio managers would only recommend voices they trusted, as otherwise it might reflect badly on them. Clients trusted the studios because they had a long relationship with them and liked to work with a specific studio. If they were not happy with a studio they would go to another one. The same thing is of course valid today.

In the '80s and '90s and now in the twenty-first century, a large number of agencies have sprouted, and work as intermediary between the voices and the end clients. It has taken out a little bit of the personal relationship that existed between the voices, the studios and the clients, but that's the way things are done now. There are also thousands of production companies which might, at some stage, need to turn their English production into a foreign version. If they don't know where to go they will probably go to an agency, or they might ask a studio manager. It is therefore a good idea to try to get your demo to an agency and see what happens. Direct marketing to the production companies is possible, but it is time consuming. However, you only need to be lucky a few times to start building a nice client base. The advantage of having a direct client is that you will probably become quite close – if you like each other, that is. If you work well together and both sides are happy, here again you will start reaping the rewards, as a happy client will talk about you to others. These things do not happen overnight. But, with a bit of luck, you already have your bread and butter translations, so remember that you are only trying to diversify, you are not starting from nowhere; time is on your side. If you are a beginner at translating, in that case you are probably still very young and you also have time though, I know, you also need to make ends meet! I have always worked at trying to build lasting relationships with clients. Many have become friends; it is a very pleasant way to work. But here again all this takes a long time and you might want to get your new venture going a bit faster!

Well, I see some big changes on the horizon. I cannot say I like them, but that is totally irrelevant to the situation. With the advent of the Internet and the market becoming global, there are many companies and individuals trying to do business on the World Wide Web. So it is becoming almost an obligation to advertise on the Web. To do that you will need to create a website; you might of course already have one. I know that many of you have bought one or designed one yourselves. In such a case it is of course very easy to add a couple of pages advertising your new services. One page for your voice-over translating and that could be a simple text. Of course, if you have gone one stage further you could also have an MP3 giving potential clients a chance to hear your voice, and if you work in vision, why not have a good picture of yourself looking at the camera, or even a video clip?

If you surf the Internet you will have noticed that there are many sites you could join free of charge or for a fee so that your name and your voice can be found by clients looking for a voice. I have grave doubts about many of these sites. I do find it difficult when the only contact you have is a large computer. You cannot speak to people, you don't know where the clients are, it is a totally impersonal way of doing business. I do not like it at all, as for the clients it is also a gamble, because they really don't have much of an idea about the skills and the talents of the voice they are using. They might listen to a very acceptable thirty seconds recording, but what they don't know is that the recording session took three hours and that the director worked very hard to extract these thirty seconds from the voice. The real recording via ISDN might turn out to be a nightmare. Of course the attraction for the client is that these types of voices will probably charge very little, undermining the market in the process.

That sort of thing has happened in the past. I remember a client outside London who did not want to use me because I wanted to charge him the same price I charged clients in London. He did not want to pay for the travel either. I stuck to my guns and one day I had this frantic phone call at about twelve o'clock. This guy wanted me to come to his studio as soon as possible to do a one-hour session. I reminded him of my cost! And he said, "Yes, of course no problem, if you can make it by one o'clock, that would really be helpful!" I jumped on my motorbike and arrived a couple of minutes before one. A secretary took me to an upstairs room where a French client and an English gentleman speaking good French made me listen to a French narration. It was terrible, a script read by someone who had never done it before; who was uneducated to the point that even the Englishman could hear there was a serious problem. I did not say anything and waited for them to tell me what they wanted me to do. So they started to tell me how I should read each sentence. When I realised what they were doing, I suggested that we go to the studio and that I would read it "My Way" and that they could stop me at anytime if there was something they did not like. The adrenaline was pumping hard through my entire body. I knew what had happened, of course. My client had asked a French person off the street to do a job that he could not do, and I do not blame the guy, he did not know better. So we worked on the levels, the English was at the right level in my ears, the return of my voice was perfect and I started to read. I did not get stopped; I did not fluff for the full ten minutes of the recording. When I came out of the booth, the clients stood up, clapped and shook my hand. I must admit I savoured the moment. I said, "Thank you very much, a piece of cake!" The studio owner was nowhere to be seen. He obviously had blamed it all on the poor soul who had been lured by what he thought was a glamorous job.

By the way, I have not mentioned this before, but the work of the voice is not really glamorous, it is very much anonymous work, like the work of the translator. Unless you translate a book, your name is almost never acknowledged and the same thing happens to voices. If you watch a very good documentary on the continent, something which has been made by BBC Bristol[1] for example, you will see a very English name in front of the word "Narration" on the end credits! If you believe the credits you would think that John Smith was a fantastic linguist without any trace of a foreign accent in dozens of languages. Even if we don't do it for public recognition that does make it harder to make a name for yourself in the business.

Anyway, marketing through the Internet is a reality and is becoming more important by the day. Clients might not get the deal they thought they would when they first made contact with a voice in Cyberspace, but the voice might also be conned as it is very difficult to know where to turn if your client does not pay you, and you don't even really know where they are. So, I would suggest a pre- or part payment in advance via Paypal for example for foreign work might be a good idea, and a good way to protect yourself. Also be suspicious if all a potential client will provide is a mobile phone number and a hotmail address.

Having said that, there have always been crooks around and knowing their address might not be so helpful either! There are of course messages circulating on the Internet about people who are not to be trusted, but it is quite often a bit late if you have been hit. Do not forget to check their websites to have a bit more info on them, but here again, one can be easily fooled. You might remember the British TV series *Hustle* where a bunch of absolutely charming conmen and one conwoman are experts at using IT to present a fantastic front and fool people into thinking they are dealing with a really solid and trustworthy organisation. I suppose I am probably deluding myself when I think knowing people is a guarantee they will pay their bills. In fact the worst two cases when I lost large amounts of money were people I had worked with over many years, one for nineteen years and another one for six years. The relationships between myself and the directors were good, but when hard times befell them, they did not give me any warning and went into liquidation before they paid me. But I must also say that one of them gave me a lead for another very big job a few months later and I almost recouped what I had lost with him in one go. So, on balance, I still prefer to work with people I know!

The ball is in your court and you will most probably have to use the Internet to find your clients. It is still early days and I hope that over time it will also be possible to develop longstanding relationships that have been started that way.

Until not so long ago, I would have said that telephoning a

few well selected people in production companies might have been a good way to enlarge your client base. Indeed, I did just that in the mid-'90s, I spent two days calling people, probably not more than one hundred calls and I found a director who was looking for someone to help him with foreign versions. We worked over many years on the very good films that he made (until he stopped making them). Those two days of telephoning had been greatly rewarding. Today I am not so sure it would work. I have received so many unsolicited phone calls in the last couple of years that I do my best to get my telephone numbers removed from directories, even specialist ones, and I have registered my numbers with a number of organisations to try to bar unwanted calls. I found that many organisations use these directories, or even ads that you might have put somewhere, to find your numbers, and then phone to offer their services or try to sell you something. I cannot recall anyone phoning me to buy my services after having found my number in a telephone directory or on an advert I might have been foolish enough to put in a publication. Advertising certainly does not seem to work for our type of translation services. It might contribute to give the company a presence on the market and build an image, but does not bring easily measurable rewards in the short term.

Here again writing an old-fashioned letter and sending it courtesy of the Royal Mail might work, but does anybody read these letters when they arrive in an office? I file most of them "vertically", in other words, I drop them in the dustbin and I have a strong suspicion that most companies do the same thing. Large companies which send hundreds of thousands of letters of this nature through the post might get a two per cent return and that might be enough to keep them in business. However, I am not sure we as one man/woman bands should spend too much time and energy on these types of activities.

Very much depending on your personality and the way you like to do things, "networking" is another tool you might want to explore. Not everybody likes to meet a lot of new people hoping to find someone who is going to lead to some work.

However, it is certainly a good way to promote your work. You only need to make yourself available and print some business cards. The easy bit is the making of the business cards. You can probably do them on your computer yourself if you have a colour printer. The difficult bit is to make yourself available. Not only do you have to spend hours sweating on translations, running to studios to make your recordings, but you might also have a family and you need to pick up the children from school or take them to their ballet lessons. Yes, life is tough if you are parents, but you need to make time to promote your business. Time management is something you should look at very carefully. You should ask yourself a few questions. Do I need to do that or that? Do I do this activity in the most efficient way? Why do I have to spend thirty minutes taking the children to school by car when I could do it in thirty minutes on foot and therefore not to have to go for a compulsory thirty minutes walk at another time during the day, just to keep fit? You can see here the "green" coming out of me! Look carefully at your day and at the way you handle each task. By finding more efficient ways of doing things you not only gain time you can use to do your marketing, or whatever else you want, but you also reduce your stress and your entire life could benefit from it.

Whatever you decide to do to sell your services, the one rule to remember is that you must do it all the time. You should not wait until you have no work to start writing letters, making phone calls, networking or updating your website. You must do it every day, even if it is for only a few minutes. It is no good doing a lot of marketing when you have no work to do. You should not find yourself in a position when you have no translations on your plate. To be in such a situation where you have work all the time, you must always be looking for clients; you must be marketing every day.

The big question is of course, "Do I want to be working all the time?" Well, this is for you to decide: you know how much money you need to lead the life you want to lead. It will all depend on how much you enjoy your work, how much time you want to spend working and how much time you want to spend on the other things in your life! It is a difficult balance to maintain. The reason it is so difficult is that on the one hand if you have too much work, you will have no time to spend on the other parts of your life and on the other hand, if you start to say no to clients because you want to keep time for yourself, you might lose the client all together.

Here again it will depend on your relationship with the client. Is it someone who employs many translators in your own language combination, or is it someone who relies almost exclusively on you? If the client is used to working with many translators in your language pair, there is no real problem in saying "no" for one job, as he or she will not feel let down and will go to one of the other translators to get the job done. However, if clients do not require your services regularly (as is often the case with voice-over translations), they might be a bit upset if they have to start looking for someone else. In the voice-over field clients can require translations very often, but they might not always be in the same languages, so these types of clients (even though they provide a lot of work to translators) do not necessarily need your services every week. If you specialise in translating voice-overs, you do not really want to lose these clients, so you have to tread carefully when you decide to say "no". If you work exclusively for voice-overs you will need to have a few hundred clients to keep you afloat. You will need to keep in touch, even if they do not give you work every year. I have just had a job, translation, voicing and recording in my own studio from a client in a production company who had not done any foreign versions for almost ten years. You therefore need to keep your address book very much up-to-date if you do not want to lose clients like this one. Be patient, carry on sending them your best wishes for the New Year. You might think that it is not worth it to get one job like this, but it is. I mention this job because it is a bit extreme and also because it is the latest job to happen. In fact I get contacted all the time by clients who have not given me any jobs for years. There are suddenly a few weeks or months of intense activity with

them, and then they stop having foreign language requirements...
well, at least until the next time...

Marketing might make a difference to the speed at which you
acquire new clients but, to conclude, I still think that the best
marketing tool is your work and I would like to end quoting this
well known saying: "*Actions speak louder than words*". If the work
you do is good, it will be appreciated by your clients, and with
time you will be known and have enough work to keep you in
business and lead a happy life.

---

1   BBC Bristol has acquired a well deserved reputation around the world
    for the quality of its documentaries on natural life.

THE FEES

I am not going to give you prices as such, but only a few hints at what is going on in the market. The market is global and we are therefore confronted with severe competition. Having said that, it is for you to decide if you want to compete on prices alone or on other criteria. It was the German chancellor, Otto von Bismark, who coined the word *Realpolitik* when dealing with the power struggle between the European Empires in the nineteenth century. Another Chancellor, Willy Brandt, was also an advocate of it during the Cold War. Principles, ideologies were at stake, but he was confronted with the everyday running of West Germany and he had to compromise. Even though, as a matter of principle I would go for quality, I had to put *de l'eau dans mon vin* (water in my wine) as the French saying goes and I have also had to compromise sometimes on prices.

The pound Sterling is very high at the time of writing and has been for a few years, which makes us expensive for potential clients outside the Sterling area. When that sort of thing happens, one must decide if lowering the price to be at the level of the local market in which your client is working is a good move or not. Are you going to "catch" clients this way? Will you be able to build a relationship and then slowly increase your prices? Is the volume of work high enough to warrant this policy? Are you hoping Sterling is going to go down or the other currency is going to go up? All these have to be taken into consideration when you establish your pricing policy. Nothing is set in stone, and you might very well decide after a little while that it was not a very good idea to lower your prices too much, and put them up again. This rise in your prices might encourage clients, if they are only interested in the cheapest product, to look for someone else. All this will depend on the amount of work you have and if you can afford to drop a client who does not pay what you would like.

As a translator you are certainly aware of all this, but as a voice, there are a number of other factors to take into consideration when you set your fee for a job. When I say "you set your fee", you might in fact not have to do that as such, as it might very well be the client who is going to make an offer. It will then be for you to decide whether you want to try to negotiate a better deal or to accept the offer. To evaluate the fee, the first thing to establish is the length of the recording session. You will then base your studio fee (BSF: Basic Studio Fee) on the number of hours or days and the regularity of the work provided by a given client. On the clients' side, once they have recognised that you are the right voice for the job, your fee might also be dictated by the number of words you can record in one hour and for how long you can go on without stumbling. You would be expected to read your script and listen back to it within one hour for a ten to fifteen minutes film. If the recording is "wild", that is when there isn't any time constraint and you are not listening to a guide track then you would reasonably record 2,500 words in one hour. This is an average.

While I have mentioned that sometimes it is possible to record 4,000 to 4,500 words an hour, this is not usual. When that happens the scripts tend to be very similar and there is rarely a new word that would make one stumble or fluff. The number of hours you will be asked to stay in the studio will very much depend on your own fitness and experience. You might think you could record for eight hours a day, but you must remain consistent all the way through and sound the same at six in the evening as you did in the morning. Most directors will split days so that no single voice works for more than three or four hours on the trot. If you are recording a play or a language course the situation is different and you will be booked all day, but you will not be reading all day. There will be plenty of time when you will not be the one doing the acting, and you will be able to rest while the other voices are working. In such a situation you will not command the same fees as if you were doing the voice work alone, reading all day long with only short breaks every hour and an hour for lunch.

For audio books the fees are paid per day or per half-day, the average number of words read could vary greatly depending on the artist and the difficulty of the script. Along the same lines and for the same sort of fees you can include the ADRs I mentioned earlier. You might very well be booked for a full day and only work five minutes in one little scene or you might be very active all day long and still earn the same amount of money. There are no repeat fees or buyout for these types of sessions. I remember once when four of us, all Frenchmen, voiced the entire *Grande Armée* of *Napoléon* marching on Moscow. We shouted all afternoon *Vive l'Empereur* for an episode of *Sharpe* for British television. The reason we had to do that was that the film was shot in one of the ex-soviet republics and that the men did not sound too convincing at being French, so by adding our French voices to the soundtrack the director added some local colour and made the story a little bit more believable. The reason the film was shot in the Ukraine, I think, was that the producers could have a very large army of men for very little money and did not have to use special effects to make a hundred men look like a million which is a trick commonly used nowadays. You can shoot a hundred people in the foreground and use for example a green backing. You then move the hundred people back, making sure they change places. The first line of them goes where the green cloth was and you have already doubled the number of people on a square, and you can do that a few times. I witnessed this very process done for the film I mentioned before, *The Flying Scotsman,* shot in 2005.

You will probably be more inclined to give a discount now and again to a regular client than to a new one. Well at least that is my point of view. On the other hand, one could argue that by giving a discount to new clients for the first job, you show what you can do and have a lot of work from them after this initial job. That could be a slippery slope, because someone else could come in and offer to do the job for even less money. If that voice is really bad, you will probably not lose that client, but if the voice is not that bad or if the client cannot tell the difference, you might very well have started a downwards trend that might be impossible to reverse. Also when you set a fee, even if you say it is at a discount you will find it almost impossible to increase it in the current climate.

What your recording is going to be used for is the second factor you will need to investigate. Many of the recordings we do are for in-house training, in other words are going to be shown to a non-paying audience. The key words here are "non-paying audience"! In that case, you will negotiate a session fee and your voice could be heard by generations of employees in a company and you will not receive a penny more. Your voice might very well be known by millions of people, but as I said before you should not expect recognition. Every now and again we have to record something which is going to be shown to a "fee-paying audience"; in this case an additional fee could be negotiated. This could cover quite a number of situations and I might very well forget some. The classification of "paying" and "non-paying" is not always easy to make. Television or radio broadcasts are considered as "fee-paying". The viewer pays the licence fee or a subscription to a television channel, or you are advertising a product which is going to make lots of money for your client. I am of course talking here about commercials. I know, I have mentioned a few times that as translators, you will probably never be asked to do a commercial but you might be both very good and very lucky and have the opportunity to do one. Or you might be an actor reading this! You therefore need to know that under these circumstances you should be paid an additional fee.

Here it becomes pretty complicated! If your recording is going to be broadcast in Great Britain, you will be paid a percentage of the session fee; it is the usage fee, the fee the client will have to pay to actually use your voice. For television they are called TVRs (Television Rights). This is all very well regulated by Equity (this is the short name of The British Actors Equity, that is the Actors Union). To find out more about Equity you can log on the following site: http://www.equity.org.uk. Equity signs agreements whenever possible with the big boys/girls in the industry on these matters very regularly. You can find out more about usage fees on the following site: http://www.usefee.tv. On the same site you will also have some guidance for the rights you might expect if your voice is used in other territories. In this case you will not receive TVRs but you will negotiate a "buyout". Depending on the size of the country the percentage of the session fee will be increased or decreased. The percentage is based on the number of potential viewers or listeners in the country concerned and therefore the number of potential buyers.

For radio in Great Britain, you will also need to contact Equity to find out how much you might get for usage. Of course you might very well work through an agent who will know and will try to obtain as much as possible for you. Agents work on commission of typically between fifteen and twenty per cent in London, so it is in their interest to obtain the highest possible fee for you.

There are quite a number of other usage fees which come into a grey area. You might be doing some voicing that is going to be used on the Internet for example, but here again will it be used only by the employees of a large corporation or will it be available to the public at large? Depending on the response, you might win an additional fee. You might record an instruction CD or a DVD which is going to be given free to people buying say, a vacuum cleaner. I do not take this example at random; we actually did record an instruction video which lasted for almost two hours. I don't know if the company selling it did well, but the vacuum cleaner seemed so complicated to use that it would have put me off buying it in the first place! On top of it, the price at the time was more than a thousand pounds which I thought would have been enough of a deterrent. I mention this only to say that in that specific case, we were paid for the recording session which was quite long, but that there was no usage fee, as the client pointed out they were not selling the video, it was "an additional bonus" for the client. Indeed, I think you would be very lucky if you obtained a usage fee for that sort of thing. What about on-board announcements for airlines? They are in a cut-throat business nowadays, and I have not been able to get usage fees for that, or if it has happened in the past it would not have been much and it is certainly not very common.

As for announcements onboard ferries, they are even less well-paid! Don't ask me why, I stopped doing those years ago! We have also been involved in recording voices for toy manufacturers who put voices into their products – sometimes you even need to sing. These have been very reasonable and a buyout has been negotiated on top of the session fee. Some voices will also record in-store announcements. These, in my experience, are notoriously badly paid, but if you are asked to update them every week or more often and if you have your own ISDN studio you might very well find it profitable to do them. The same goes for commercials for local radio stations which are paid very little money for one commercial, but if you are an actor, and here I think you really need to be very good with your voice, you might be doing dozens of voices a day and it then becomes quite profitable. I remember once being told by a match seller that you could make a fortune selling matchsticks; I was gazing at a poor-looking soul selling his boxes for 3d at the time. (It was before decimalisation in Great Britain. This is a date I will not forget as the decimalisation of the currency was the first story I had to write for the BBC in the winter of '71, just a few days after I came back from a visit to Ireland where I had duly kissed the Blarney Stone, situated near Cork![1]) He then explained that if for every ten boxes he sold he was making 1d, it would be 100,000d if he managed to sell a million boxes!

Now let's look at the delicate problem of payment. By law all payments should be made within thirty days, but it rarely happens. Some agencies and companies manage to do it and it is great. However, many just do not have the cash flow required to achieve this target. Many small companies have to wait to be paid before they pay their suppliers or subcontractors themselves. In the film industry, agents have a client account and pay within ten days of their invoice being settled. Agents mainly operate a "self billed" system whereby they invoice on behalf of their client (the voice or the actor), and pay them back less their commission. It is a good idea to keep track of your invoices so that you always know what is outstanding. Always keep a record of the work you do for an agency, even if you do not send them an invoice. I am not saying that agencies are dishonest, but if it is a very large one, they might lose track of your account.

For example, I recorded a commercial in October 2004; after a couple of months I was paid the session fee, but there was no sign of the TVRs and I had to remind the agency to chase up the client for the money. The TVRs were not paid until the following August! So do keep a record of what you are doing or you might lose money without realising it. A good policy is to send a reminder or a statement after the thirty days. Invoices do get lost in the system from time to time, however well organised a company is, or they get lost in the post. It is therefore better to double-check after the thirty days just to make sure that your invoice is being processed properly and that your client is aware that you are expecting payment. It is also a good incentive for your clients to put pressure on their own clients.

In our business, like in many others I expect, there are a number of intermediaries and the larger the number of them the longer it takes to be paid. If you have so called *direct* clients in the industry the payment time will vary greatly as well. Some large corporations are very good at paying as they do not have to wait for payment themselves, some others are very greedy and like to make money by holding on to your payment as long as possible. In my experience, payments have been made a bit faster in the last few years. The delays were very long in the '80s and early '90s when interest rates were reaching peaks of fifteen per cent. People with money wanted to keep it for as long as possible in their bank account as it produced high returns, and small companies with cash flow problems and large debit accounts could not afford to increase their overdraft. Delays were very long then and there were many bankruptcies as well, which affected many sole traders and small companies in our industry. Apart from a few clients who still take ages to pay, most of them seem to pay within two months at the moment which is a great improvement.

With the internationalisation of trade, we also have to deal with clients abroad; it is not harder to obtain payment from them than it is from clients in your own country. I have found through the years that if clients do not want to pay, for whatever reason, they will not pay. You might take them to court, but they will either fight the case which you might win or lose, but, even worse, they might not be bothered and by the time the bailiffs arrive on their premises they will have disappeared; at least that is what I experienced in the '80s and '90s. There is also the dreaded letter arriving from the liquidators advising you that the client you have been chasing for months is going into liquidation. In thirty years in business with about a dozen clients going into liquidation, I have only been paid once, a few pounds from the company's assets, and that was back in 1976. It has never happened again. Once the preferential creditors have been paid, there is nothing left for you. If there is some money left, it seems quite extraordinarily to be equal to the amount of money due to the liquidators! Here again this is what I have seen in the few cases I have experienced in my years in business.

Having said all that, and having gone through difficult times when clients did not pay and yet we still had to to pay suppliers, the overall situation over a period of thirty years has been good and the losses have been relatively small. You will find that if you do not have subcontractors or suppliers, your business situation will not be too bad, even if one of your clients does not pay. To be in a relatively safe situation it might be wise to try to have a number of clients rather than one big one who could of course disappear suddenly pulling the carpet from under your feet. It is a policy I have tried to follow and which has served me well. Leaving my employer, the BBC in 1980, I did not want to find myself in a situation where I would depend on only one supplier. However prestigious the company you work for, you could be made redundant for all sorts of reasons and find yourself out of work. Five years after I had left Bush House, the French service was drastically curtailed and many of my ex-colleagues found themselves on the dole. This is exactly why, as a freelance you do not want to be confronted with the same problem by relying on a single client.

It is sometimes possible to ask for advance payment when you start a large project with a client you have never worked with before or if this client is situated abroad. You might state in your terms that you want to have thirty per cent with the order, thirty per cent on delivery and the last forty per cent within one month. This is when you discover how trustworthy your new client is. If the first instalment arrives with the order, this is indeed a good sign. I remember a case not that long ago when a director wanted one of his documentaries to be dubbed in a number of foreign languages. This client had been recommended by a satisfied customer for whom we had done some work on similar high standard documentaries. However, as he was based abroad I thought it might not be a bad idea to state our terms before going any further as the amount of money involved was large and there were going to be many subcontractors, translators and actors. It turned out that this director did not have the money; he was hoping to string us along until he had recovered his costs selling the documentaries before paying us. Well, that is all very well if you are the producers of the documentaries, but not if you are supplying services. There is no reason you should be financing someone else's business if you are not going to reap the profits as well, so beware.

With clients abroad, there are a number of options, like accepting payments by credit card, but that is a costly operation. The setting-up is expensive, the quarterly rentals are high and of course the bank takes a commission as well, so this is probably not a very good option. There are Internet options like Paypal. I have not joined them yet, but I know many voices and translators who have. It is a way to guarantee payment at minimum cost to both sides. And there are probably other options on the Web that you might consider to facilitate payment of your services.

---

1   According to tradition the Blarney Stone bestows the gift of the gab to the one who kisses it!

MAKING
A DEMO

As a voice artiste you will need to make a demo to show potential clients what you can do. This can take many different forms. When I first started, you did not really have any demos, you just turned up to the studio and were judged on your merit. If you were no good, that was it! If you were good, your name was added to the studio address book, which was a book into which you actually wrote with a pen or a biro. The studio would then recommend you to their clients in need of a voice. I am talking here about foreign voice artistes more than English ones who tended to be actors (more or less well known) who got the jobs from their agents. But then came the cassette recorder and everything changed. Production companies wanted to hear the voices; they realised there were different types of foreign voices and that it would be nice to offer their clients a choice. It was made possible by cassettes and I have still a specially designed shelf with hundreds of cassettes from foreign voices going back to the early '80s, some of them long gone into retirement or even more permanently. I just cannot get rid of these obsolete cassettes. Yes, I do thrive on nostalgia, mea culpa. I think it makes me feel good to delve into the old times, to listen to old records and watch old films, from even before I was born.

As you might have gathered if you have read so far, it does not stop me using modern technology, I find it a challenge and as such very stimulating! But back to the demo! With the advent of the demo and the explosion in the number of production companies, the market changed. A large number of voice agencies saw an opportunity and seized it: the cassettes made it easier for them to "sell" their voices. DATs were used as well to send demos, but they were and still are expensive tapes and you needed a special DAT recorder to produce them in house. If you go to a studio it is quite dear as well, but of course the DAT quality is superb! Because of the costs involved, the DAT was not used that much by voices to produce their demos. The cassettes were slowly overtaken by CDs instead and now "everyone who intends to make it in the world of the voice-over needs to have a demo CD". Well, I am not so sure about that, I think that the CD will become obsolete as well very soon. They are still used but you will also need to have MP3 files to send to your clients. They are small; they are easily stored, and can be sent around the world in minutes rather than days.

Many agencies did not know the voices in person and still don't. They go by the demo and if the demo is good, they assume the artist is good. I have grave doubts about this because I have received many CDs which seemed to be fantastic with endless tracks of commercials being recorded. In fact so many that I started to wonder why I did not quite recognise these voices from radio or from television. If this guy has done so many high-profile commercials, he must certainly be well known? It is then that I discovered a couple of things. Potential voice artistes spent many hours in studios, spending a fortune, to make all these commercials, well "mock commercials", which have never been broadcast of course. There were also some narrations, technical or otherwise. Once I discovered this, I started to audition people, asking them to come to my office for a meeting to get acquainted and also to ask them to read for me. In many cases, these people are not really able to read more than three words and they very often cannot make sense of the sentence. I have spent a lot of time with people telling them what to do if they wanted to improve their reading skills. I tell them to come back for another audition when they feel ready, in three months or six months time. Well, you would be surprised, but so far none of the scores of people I have seen has ever come back.[2] It is hard work as I have mentioned before, and few people are prepared, it seems, to invest their time in improving their reading techniques: it is a pity really. We need people who can read the way I have described extensively earlier on. So, demos have to be done honestly, and if to read ten lines of narration takes the artist half an hour, you realise that there is something misleading about the demo.

I have also recently received demos which are for my purpose badly mixed; the sound effects and the music are so loud that you can hardly hear the voice. That might be quite acceptable as a production, but I would not recommend it for a foreign voice-over demo. Clients want to be able to hear the voice clearly, maybe have it double-checked to be certain that the people reading are genuinely natives of the country they pretend to be. It is very important to be a native speaker as you need to know the language inside out. As I explained earlier, there will be countless cases where you will have to direct yourself and where you will have to edit the script as you go along as well. If you are only good at reading the words if they have been well written by someone else but you cannot change them because you don't know the language well enough, then you will not really be able to do the job properly and you will not be asked to come again.

That said, you might very well be asked to read in a foreign language with your original accent. I am very often asked to read in a foreign language with my French accent. I remember dubbing a Frenchman in English, German, Italian and Spanish. It was a corporate production for a multinational and this Frenchman was a client saying how happy he was with the services this car rental company had been providing him.

Certainly my advice for a demo aimed at the corporate sector is to read some technical scripts with no music and no sound effects and not spend much money, if any, on going to a specialist studio. The choice of texts is important so that you can show the different types of reading you can do. After a very technical script about cars or medicine, you could choose a narration of a beautiful documentary on somewhere like Plivitce, in Croatia.[1] I mention this one because it is probably one of the most poignant documentaries about a nature reserve I have recorded.

However, if you wish to enter the commercials market, then

you might consider going to an expensive studio with a director to help you make your CD or your selection of MP3s that you will send on request to your potential clients. I would suggest you write your own scripts, the reason being that there are only a finite number of scripts used in studios and they might not sound too good; you will be sending your demo to the large advertising agencies, and they hear the same text being read by different people too many times. The advantage of writing your own text is that it is going to be unique and will have a stronger impact on the client. It can be funny or otherwise, the choice is yours. Of course if you have your own studio, you can record demos on request. I used to do that on my cassette recorder even in the early days. I won many jobs like that, the reason being that if a client asked me for a demo for a film about cars, I would record for them a script about cars, if they wanted to make a medical film, then I sent them a medical narration. This way, they knew straight away if I was the right voice, and very often I was, because they did not have to imagine what I would sound like when reading their own script. The best way is to ask for the client to send a paragraph or a page of the script they want to record, and do a demo of that bit. This is certainly a very good way to approach the making of demos. For all sorts of reasons clients may not send the script and you have to rely on your collection of previous scripts to send them something similar to what they want to hear. You do need to have a general demo where you can show off as much as possible. You can always send that straight away and then ask if a more specific demo is required. I would like to remind you here that you must not forget to be authoritative and friendly at the same time. A telltale sign of inexperience is the smacking of lips and the voice fading at the end of sentences.

---

1   The title of this documentary is *Land of the Falling Lakes* and was broadcast by the BBC in 2004. My French version was broadcast in France the same year.

2   I have since started charging for these sessions. The result? More serious people apply, and having done the hard work, come back.

TEAMBUILDING

I know you might think it is a bit difficult to build a team spirit if you are working on your own in front of your computer, translating your scripts and then recording them in your own studio. All this is done on your own! Or is it? Well, not quite, in my view. For starters, to keep in business you need to have clients and what I want to do is build a team spirit with my clients. It presents many advantages and not least it makes life, working life, or maybe even social life, more pleasant. By building a team spirit you make your clients as aware of your needs as you become aware of theirs. To satisfy the needs of both parties, working as a team will make the process much smoother.

For example, typically the script will arrive late, by a few hours or a few days, and that could create havoc in your schedule and the client's schedule. There is no need to be rude to the client about that sort of situation, it happens all the time, it is part of business life – things are delayed on the way. Your clients have their own clients to satisfy and they depend on other suppliers to deliver on time so that you can get your script as promised. There is not much point in trying to find someone to blame. If you work as a team with your clients they will do their utmost to keep to the schedule, and they know that if they don't they will have to give you a bit more time. They will only know that if you have been speaking to them and explaining that you cannot sit and wait for their script to arrive on your desk, that you have other commitments, unless of course they are prepared to pay for you to wait, which does not happen very often. On the other hand, you will try to help them by catching up for them. Well, yes, you have other commitments, but with a bit of luck you can start on something else while you are waiting for them; this together with the little bit more time you might have obtained from them will mean that the team as a whole can succeed. Of course you do not want it to be a one-way process: you give a bit, and they give a bit. One of the reasons clients expect the translations to be done very fast is that they do not understand the nature of the work. This is why you need to spend time educating them, if I may put it this way. If you explain the difficulties of translating, that it is not a question of replacing an English word with another one, but that it is much more complex, they will start to understand that you need time to work well. You also need to show them that it is to their benefit to help you as much as possible in producing the best translations. Remind them that when the original script was written there was a lot of to-ing and fro-ing between the different people involved in writing it, and that there should be some collaboration between the translator and the writer of the original script, for example. All this explaining needs to be done long before the pressure is on and the work needs to be delivered quickly. If you have left the explaining to the time the script arrives late, you are in trouble, your client is in trouble, in other words, the team spirit is not there and the project is under threat. It is therefore important to build your team.

There is yourself, there is your client and there is the writer. There might be an agency involved in between as well. A face-to-face meeting with clients could bring huge dividends. Of course I am not talking about meeting someone for a translation of 200 words, but if the project is big enough and is going to be ongoing it is well worth the time.

I have recently been involved with a project where the video film is going to be between thirty and forty minutes long and there are going to be four issues a year plus a number of special editions. This project involves quite a bit of work as both voice-over translations and subtitling will be required in over ten languages. To organise these successfully and put all the chances on our side, we decided to have a meeting of the main people concerned. Two came from abroad, the person in charge of subtitling came, and I was also invited by the director of the recording studio to attend. The benefits of such a meeting are numerous: first, we were able to establish all the technical parameters everyone had to respect to make sure all the hardware and software would be compatible. (This of course could have easily been done by an exchange of e-mails.) Secondly, by meeting face to face, it was easy for all of us to make the other participants aware of everyone's needs. This was the point where I could explain the translators' requirements and the minimum time required to do the job properly. I was also able to obtain the contacts of all the people within the company who could help and who were going to sign off the translations before they were recorded as voices or subtitles.

We were told that one of them was especially difficult and always complained about the translations sent to him. We therefore decided that it would be a good idea for the translator of that specific language to have a chat with this "important" individual in the company so that they could establish a rapport. The experience with this person had been that he always complained generally about the quality of the translations sent to him, but was never able to produce a document detailing his complaints. In such a situation, all sorts of thoughts can come to mind, and it is impossible to find out what is wrong with the translation or the man responsible to vet it. It was not that the translations were bad; they were double-checked by other specialists, the translators were changed, but the translations were never to his liking. The man complaining was of course blaming an anonymous translator, an entity named "translator" like a faulty machine not doing quite what one would expect.

Once the contact had been established between the translator and the "important" man in the company, suddenly things changed for the better. The translator had a general conversation asking about the sort of style the "important" man wanted, he also asked him if he could possibly call him if there were any doubts in his mind about a word or a sentence. In other words, he made him part of the team, not someone who had to criticise systematically from his ivory tower. Instead of criticising, he was able to be part of the project from the start and work with the translator and not against him. This time I said "him" because it is indeed a man who handled this situation. As a team, problems become much easier to resolve and work becomes much more rewarding.

THE ALEXANDER
TECHNIQUE

I realised I had to do something about my back in 1985. That year I decided for all sorts of reasons to start riding a motorbike and also riding horses. I had had problems with my back before. It had been extremely painful and was put right by a strong physiotherapist who unblocked my vertebrae. I therefore decided that the way to do it was to strengthen the muscles in my back by going to a gym and also to sit up properly at my desk or behind the microphone. I went to the gym very seriously for only a year but I have never stopped being aware of how I sit.

There was a fantastic machine at the gym, certainly absolutely fantastic for me. (I had tried Yoga in the past, but never really enjoyed it. However, I liked doing the candle, and although painful on the neck, this is of course compensated by the good feeling it creates in the rest of the body.) This machine is a sort of scale on which you strap your ankles. You then lie on it and you slowly (sometimes not so slowly if it has not been calibrated properly for your height) turn upside-down. The weight of all your internal organs is always pressing downwards, so when you are upside-down there is an incredible feeling of relief going through your body. The machine at the gym broke and the manager did not want to buy a new one pretending that nobody was using it. I said I was using it; it did not make any difference, so I did not renew my subscription and bought a machine for myself that I am still using.

Using this machine regularly had an astonishing effect. I went for a medical after about a year of use and the nurse measured me and said, "One metre seventy-two and a half!" I asked if she could use another height gauge. She was a bit astonished but we went into the doctor's room and we tried again and she said, "One metre seventy-two and a half!" Well I had grown two and half centimetres in a year. That is just over one inch! The last time I had been measured, and that was official as it was in my passport, was at the time I did my National Service when I measured one metre seventy exactly. So by using this contraption my spine had been redressed so to speak. My vertebrae were not squashing my disks together and my back was very happy! If you have one of these machines you can use it at any time, preferably before having a meal, while for ladies it is not recommended during

their periods. A Yoga teacher also told me that when you are upside down, you should not close your eyes. One word of warning: when you come back to the normal standing-up position, do not do it too fast as it could make you faint. I find it very relaxing to spend a couple of minutes in the horizontal position, before standing up and going back to my desk.

To teach myself what a good sitting position is, I also acquired a Back Chair, one of these strange-looking seats on wheels, with no rest for the back and where the weight of the body rests on the knees. It forces one to keep the back straight. Never use that seat for more than fifteen or twenty minutes at a time, as recommended by the manufacturers, because after a little while your knees start to hurt. All these "tricks" worked very well for me as I have not had any back problems since. I did have a stiff neck at one point when I started riding the motorbike because of the weight of the helmet, but that soon disappeared and I do not seem to suffer from anything in that region of the body. I would like to give you another example of the importance of doing things the right way to improve your health. At one stage I developed a "tennis elbow" and was not altogether surprised as I was playing tennis. However, I was probably overdoing it a bit as I was also fencing and using a computer mouse. They are three activities which demand a lot of the right arm in my case.

I first stopped fencing as I prefer outside sports when I come out of the office or the studio, rather than being inside again. I started using the mouse late; I preferred to use shortcuts on the keyboard. I was not using it very much and I realised that I was

not doing what had been recommended, i.e. I did not rest my forearm properly on the desk when using the mouse. I therefore decided to correct that and made sure that every time I used the mouse I would rest my arm properly on the desk. Being rather a radical person, I also thought as the use of the mouse was not a very difficult activity that I would use my left hand, which tends to be under used by right-handers. It did not take me very long to become totally at ease with using my right-hand mouse with my left hand. The advantage of not having reconfigured the mouse to be used by a real left-hander is that most other people coming to my desk can use the mouse without having to struggle

because the buttons have been inverted. I gave up tennis for a little while and when the pain had gone I decided I would go about playing tennis the proper way if that was possible at all and I asked Floyd the tennis coach in our local park to show me how to hold the racket properly. I re-educated myself in using the proper grip for the proper stroke, my tennis improved no end and my tennis elbow seems to be history.

Like everybody, with old age creeping in, I get a painful Achilles tendon and muscle pains when I think I am still twenty and stay on the tennis courts for too long! *"The spirit is willing but the flesh is weak!"* I am not sure it was meant in that context but never mind; this is exactly what happens to me!

I discovered by myself that exercising and a good sitting position were good for the body and the soul, *"mens sana in corpore sano"*. I was only reinventing the wheel, which is a typical French trait. This is what I realised when I was introduced to The Alexander Technique by a good friend who teaches this method – a very different approach to how we use ourselves in everything we do in our daily lives.

The Alexander Technique teaches you how to avoid unnecessary strain in everyday activities, leading to greater freedom and ease of movement.

But first who was Frederick Matthias Alexander and why and how did he develop his technique? I must say that I liked the character when I started to hear about him. I suppose it is not surprising as he was himself a performer. He was born in Tasmania in 1869 and developed very early on a liking for reciting. He went straight for the great speeches

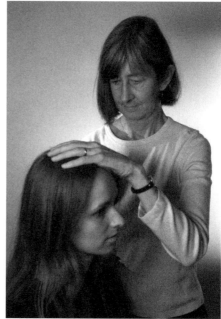

An Alexander Technique teacher and a pupil

by Shakespeare. In those days, as there were no amplification systems in the great halls, actors had to have a stentorian voice to be heard. Actors had to master the art of projection to the full and had to do it in such a way that they would not break their voice. Projecting yes but not shouting. The sound had to come from right deep down; it was not and is not possible to use the throat, as it would not last for very long, to produce a loud sound. Alexander was perfectly *au fait* with all that, but it did not stop him losing his voice! Nothing worse could have befallen a man in his profession. He went to see a number of doctors and specialists, but apart from giving him some syrups and asking him to rest his voice they didn't know why he had a problem.

Well, that was not good enough for Alexander who didn't want to abandon his career that easily. The doctors not being able to help, he decided he had to find out for himself the whys and wherefores of his condition. Thinking about his problem, he came to the conclusion that it might be something he was doing when he was reciting on stage that was the cause of the problem. He couldn't very well film himself and study his performance the way sportsmen do nowadays, to find out what went wrong or indeed what worked and how this could be repeated.

His solution was to watch himself in a mirror. That is how he saw that he was pulling his head backwards when he was speaking. He had not realised that he was doing that, so he looked carefully to see if there was anything else he was doing that might contribute to his problem. By looking at himself in the mirror he also became more aware of his posture and attitude and found out that he was doing a number of things he was not doing when he was speaking to friends. By carefully looking at himself in the mirror he went on to discover other things, like his legs starting to stiffen and that he was pushing his toes into the floor, arching his spine and lifting his chest. So he slowly worked at modifying his stance to ease the pressure on the spine, by letting the head go forward and up rather than back. He realised that if his head was in balance the spine could achieve its full length. Through the study of his own body he managed to cure himself of his problem and was able to declaim again on stage without losing his voice anymore. However, his study of his own use of himself took over from his love of reciting, and he wrote four books on the subject from 1910 to 1941. Despite some scepticism from doctors to start with, before long many admitted that Alexander had really hit on a winner. Alexander realised that as adults we develop "bad habits" and lose the alertness seen in babies and young children. Relearning the "good habits" of youth leads to improved well-being, both mentally and physically. The philosophers of old knew that already, but Alexander turned it into a technique.

His holistic approach to improving the way we use ourselves has now been recognised by many and his work carried on after his death. The Society of Teachers of the Alexander Technique (STAT) was founded in 1958 and there are now thousands of teachers around the world. It is very difficult to explain what will happen in Alexander Technique lessons, but many actors have tried them and learnt a lot from them. It is an entire attitude to life that you are going to discover but it is going to take time and commitment to benefit from it. It is, I suppose, easier to say what it is not. It is not a miracle cure as it is not like going to the physiotherapist or the osteopath and getting your tennis elbow sorted out in a couple of sessions. One of the main messages is that your mind and body work together as one system. You will not feel light and happy if you have just learned that a close friend has died, whereas you will feel happy if you have just learnt that you have become a grandfather for the first time, to take one example.

Developing conscious awareness of how we are using ourselves affects our movement and balance, leading to improvement in how we function in all our activities. In other words we will be readier to deal both with our daily chores and the problems we face in our lives.

All this means that you will be using your body in the best possible way to achieve your aims. There are no activities I can think of that will not entail some body movements. Something as simple as reading will mean that you must hold the book and turn the pages. Even if you are reading a script on a computer screen you will have to use at least one hand to move the page on the screen down and you will also require the use of your eyes to read the text.

To try to encapsulate Alexander's technique I would say that improved use of yourselves (body and mind) will enable you to lead a fuller life.

However, you cannot learn The Alexander Technique by reading books alone; you need to meet a teacher to really find out how to do it. The easiest way to find one is to log on to the website: http://www.stat.org.uk/

CONCLUSION

If you have stayed with me this far, then you have come a long way from being a translator of the written word to a specialist of the spoken one, or from a stage actor to a voice-over specialist. You will have seen that through hard work and training you can improve your skills and acquire new ones. Translators will have a new string to their bow if they specialise in translating the spoken word and they could even start new careers as voice artists. Remember, there is a lot of competition in that field as there are many actors who are ahead of you here, but you could catch up with them by working on improving your voice.

Actors, if they happen to have a foreign language, could also develop translating skills and here again, it will not happen overnight. They will have to go through arduous work, honing their writing skills in their own language and developing a great understanding of the foreign one they have chosen to learn. There is training around; many courses are run to learn languages and to learn how to translate. The problem is the willingness of the individual to invest time and hard work to achieve the required standards. Some actors "rest" quite often in between productions; therefore in theory they should have the time to learn a new trade. In practical terms it would be ideal for some actors as they could take the translation work almost anywhere on a laptop and use some of the waiting time in this profession to write a translation. Indeed, many actors are writers in their own right and take their computers with them on locations sometimes. It is a fantastic way not to lose your spirit when there is no acting work around and you can also supplement your income this way. But actors, remember, always translate into your mother tongue, never try to do it in a foreign one! I am emphasising the word actors as I would expect professional translators to know about that.

If you have read this far, I know that you are people who like a challenge, as it is a challenge for both translators and actors. Translators are very often people who like to work on their own and who might even be a bit shy, so imagine the leap they would have to make to become a professional voice. But it can be done! This is what I have tried to explain in this book. Translators can find out easily if they can read aloud and if they can, how to improve their reading. I have also explained how to train the voice to sound convincing; furthermore, I have given information on how to build a home studio and how to market these new services. Budding actors might also benefit from the studio-reading techniques which are a bit different from what they do on stage. The appropriate behaviour in the studio is also explained in the chapter on Etiquette and should prove useful to newcomers as well as old hands who might have forgotten a thing or two.

Writing the book I have also realised that it would be very good if clients were to read it! Some would probably understand a bit more of what translators and voices are confronted with when they have to make a foreign version for them.

I think I have used a common sense approach to making foreign versions through my career and if all parties concerned were to do the same, their quality would improve dramatically to the benefit of the end client and all concerned.

BIBLIOGRAPHY

Umberto Eco: *Mouse or Rat? Translation as negotiation* – First published in GB by Weidenfeld & Nicolson in 2003

George Orwell: *Politics and the English Language* – First published in 1946

Frederick Matthias Alexander:
    Man's Supreme Inheritance, 1910
    Constructive Conscious control, 1924
    The Use of the Self, 1931
    The Universal Constant Living, 1941

Glynn Macdonald: *Alexander Technique* – First published by in GB by Elements Books Limited in 1998

"A Way of Working", article published by Mary Holland in *The Strad,* Volume 89, 1063 November 1978

Chris Stevens: *An introductory guide* – First published by Optima in 1987

INDEX

NOTES

NOTES

NOTES

NOTES

NOTES

NOTES

NOTES

NOTES

NOTES

NOTES

NOTES

NOTES